How to Use the Learning Covenant
in Religious Education

KENOSIS SERIES

Kenosis is a venerable biblical term (Phil 2:7) which orthodox Patristic exegetes interpreted as expressing the process whereby the Second Person of the Trinity emptied himself into history and took on human form. In the ongoing kenotic process, Jesus fully had two distinct but united natures, God and human. This hypostatic union always remains and can never be dissolved. In this kenotic process, the human nature of Jesus was directly and immediately sanctified by his intimate contact with his fully-functioning though usually hidden divine nature. In the kenosis, Jesus typically subjected his divine nature to the total service of his human nature in order to accomplish the two basic purposes in God's overall eschatological design: redemption and religious instruction.

Each Kenosis Book is analogous in some ways to the biblical kenosis. In the pedagogical kenosis, inexhaustible theory empties itself into the religious instruction act and takes on practical form. In this pedagogical kenosis, the religious instruction act has two distinct but interactive natures, theory and practice. This union always remains and can never be dissolved. In the kenotic process, the practice nature of the religious instruction act is directly and immediately made fruitful by its intimate contact with the usually hidden theoretical nature. In the pedagogical kenosis, the religious instructiton act subjects its theoretical dimension to the total service of practice in order to effectively achieve desired religious instruction outcomes.

How to Use
the Learning Covenant
in Religious Education:

Working with Adults

by

R. E. Y. Wickett

A Kenosis Book

Religious Education Press
Birmingham, Alabama

Library of Congress Cataloging-in-Publication Data

Wickett, R. E. Y.
    How to use the learning covenant in religious education : working
with adults / by R.E.Y. Wickett.
        p.   cm. — (A kenosis book)
    Includes bibliographical references and index.
    ISBN 0-89135-109-4 (alk. paper)
    1. Christian education of adults. 2. Learning contracts. 3. Covenants—
Religious aspects—Christianity. I. Title. II. Series.
    BV1488 .W536 1999
    268'.434—dc21
                                                                98-45966
                                                                CIP

Religious Education Press
5316 Meadow Brook Road
Birmingham, Alabama 35242-3315

10 9 8 7 6 5 4 3 2

Religious Education Press publishes books exclusively in religious education and in areas closely related to religious education. It is committed to enhancing and professionalizing religious education through the publication of serious, significant, and scholarly works.

PUBLISHER TO THE PROFESSION

CONTENTS

ILLUSTRATIONS

WHAT YOU WILL LEARN FROM READING THIS BOOK

Religious educators and learners in many parts of the world use learning covenants (or contracts) quite extensively. This book describes the basic patterns for effective use of a learning covenant in the best interests of the learner and for a successful learning process. It provides the religious educator with procedures to ensure a positive and successful learning process.

The reader will be introduced to the basic concepts of the learning covenant and the theological underpinning that supports this educational model. It is the theological aspect that distinguishes it from its secular counterpart. This book reviews (1) preparation for the covenant process, (2) covenant formation, (3) covenant implementation and monitoring, and (4) covenant evaluation. It also describes the use of learning covenants in group situations. Specific examples of learning covenants and the learning processes are provided to illuminate the principles of learning covenant relationships and the learning covenant process.

Learning covenants are valuable to the adult religious educator because they provide a vehicle for both individual and group learning activities. There are many situations in the church in which learners do not share the same learning needs and interests. A particular individual who is called to perform a specific type of ministry in a faith community or an individual who is involved in a certain part of the faith journey may have learning needs that are not shared by any other person at that time.

A covenant allows the educator to support the learner in the manner that best suits the learner's individual requirements. It provides a basis for appropriate standards and for meeting the needs of the faith community.

Some things that you will learn from reading this book include the following:

a. You will learn when this model is suitable for use with a specific learner or group of learners, when it is suitable for use with specific content, and when to use this model for either individual or group learning activities.

b. You will learn how to work cooperatively with the learner to support the development of an appropriate learning covenant. Specific references will be made to the determination of the particular focus of the learning process and the resources required to achieve the necessary results. An appropriate process for the learning will be included in the description.

c. You will learn how to monitor the learning process in order to assist the learner(s) to proceed appropriately. Certain difficulties could disrupt the learning process. This monitoring will enable you to facilitate the learner's adjustment to changing circumstances.

d. You will learn to help the learner or learners to bring closure to a successful learning experience. This process of closure will include reference to self-evaluation and any other criteria that are relevant to the process.

One difference between the two terms "covenant" and "contract" is found in the different orientations that people have to them. The word "contract" has a legalistic connotation in our society, which pays little attention to the social dimension of the term. On the other hand, the term covenant has a strong religious connotation with social and individual implications. Those who are familiar with Jewish and Christian writings will also see the spiritual dimension of the term.

A second major difference between the two educational models, covenants and contracts, involves the nature of the relationships within covenants. Covenant relationships involve the educator, the learner, and God. Contractual relationships focus on the legal relationships between individuals or groups.

The learning covenant enables us to move beyond merely human interaction and the constraints of legalistic attitudes to see learning covenants within a broader theological and social context.

2

GETTING STARTED TOWARD MASTERING THE LEARNING COVENANT

This chapter provides background information in regard to the educational model we are calling the learning covenant, which has been identified closely with the learning contract model as developed by Malcolm Knowles. Topics touched upon include a review the history of the model, the teaching/learning principles that underlie its use, and the theoretical perspectives that govern the procedure as a whole.

A HISTORY OF LEARNING COVENANTS

This section of the chapter reviews the concept of learning covenants from the perspective of both religious education and the field of education as a whole. It also describes certain theological concerns.

General Education

Educators have used formal learning covenants or contracts in a variety of settings with adult learners for the past two decades and with children and adolescents in school settings. This model is called the learning contract in the secular context.

Learning contracts were made popular in adult education

during the late 1970s and 1980s through the writings of Malcolm Knowles. His first book on the topic, *Self-Directed Learning: A Guide for Learners and Teachers*, brought the learning contract model to prominence in North America and beyond. This book was followed by a considerably revised and expanded version *Using Learning Contracts.*

The extensive use of learning contracts or covenants is documented in Knowles's writings (including *Using Learning Contracts*) and in the writings of other authors. This model has been used effectively in a wide variety of learning situations with many different groups of learners.

A useful aspect of this model is the way in which assistance is given to the learner in developing skills for independent learning. The process of planning to learn, particularly where resource identification is involved, is valuable to any learner. Educators contribute to the learners' ability to function in life by assisting them to increase the ability to perform learning activities, with support only when necessary.

I have observed the use of the learning contract model in the United States, Canada, and Great Britain with both adolescents and adults. It has proven to be effective in both secular and religious arenas.

Religious Education

I call this model the learning covenant model when it occurs in the religious education context. In religious education the learning covenant model has been used more extensively with adults than with children and adolescents. Schools tend to use the more traditional learning contract model or they may use the learning covenant as an optional model for particular material.

The learning covenant model has been used extensively with adult learners in seminaries and theological schools, which focus on training for particular forms of ordained ministry. Specific professional preparation for certain forms of ministry may be very effective through the use of the covenant model when the focus is clear and the individual's needs and abilities are known, for example, the supervised internship that many seminaries and theological schools require of their students.

Students in training for ordained ministry are often required to spend time in a supervised, practical experience of ministry, which can take place in a variety of settings including rural or urban communities, large or small faith communities, or a secular institution such as a hospital or prison chaplaincy.

The Biblical Concept of Covenant

Although there is evidence of covenants that predate the Jewish tradition, the concept of the covenant is important in both Jewish and Christian literature. My personal experience in the Christian tradition and in adult education places the focus on the biblical perspective of the New Testament. I am certain that others will place equally valid interpretations upon the concept from their own scriptural traditions.

There are numerous uses of the word "covenant" in both Old and New Testament in reference to particular relationships, and the word describes different types of relationships in different passages.

The *Interpreter's Dictionary of the Bible* describes both Old and New Testament covenants, including covenants between people and covenants that involve God and people directly. Covenants that involve God and his people are discussed most frequently in detail, but we should also be aware of the other types of covenants.

Covenants between persons of equal status were frequently used to maintain stable and peaceful relationships among groups of people. The nature of these covenants is not always described in great detail in the Bible, but we do see their implications for peace and prosperity among nations and stable relationships among important persons. The most important scriptural covenants in the view of many Jews and Christians are the ones that involve God and the collective, or "the people of God," with various interpretations of the meaning of that phrase. Both Old and New Testaments include a series of these covenants. These covenants involve certain responsibilities for both parties, as do other biblical covenants.

Old Testament covenants include those that bind God, for example, the Abrahamic covenant (Genesis 15; 17:1–14), and those that bind the people of Israel, for example, the Mosaic covenant that features the Ten Commandments (Exodus 20).

The New Testament concept of the covenant differs from the Old Testament concept but remains linked to it. For example, a connection can be seen between the comments on Christ's blood made at the Last Supper (Mathew 26:28, Mark. 14:24, Luke 22:20; and 1 Corinthians 11:25) and the "blood of the covenant" mentioned in Exodus 24:8.

The earliest Christians quite readily used the term "covenant" without its Old Testament connotations. Paul clearly indicates that this new covenant is a "covenant of the spirit" (2 Corinthians 3:6) in contrast to the Mosaic law which was clearly embodied in written form.

The letter to the Hebrews shows the changes from the old forms of covenant to the new (Hebrews 7:1–22: 8: 9:28; 12:24; 13:20) with direct references to the "new" covenant based on the death of Christ. The connection in Hebrews 13:20 clearly indicates the covenant as "everlasting," thereby demonstrating the view that the concept had integrity through its various manifestations.

The nature of the biblical covenant clearly changed as the "people of God" changed. As their experience molded their views of God, the nature of the covenant that exemplified the relationship also changed.

Theological Perspectives On Teaching/Learning Covenants

We do not find direct parallels between covenants described in the Old and New Testaments and the covenant aspect of the teaching/learning relationship. We must seek to find the key aspects from among the biblical passages and related writings. We could pursue this task by examining various dimensions of the covenant concept as outlined in figure 2.1.

The sides of the triangle represent the covenant relationships between God and the teacher, between God and the learner, and between the teacher and the learner. The latter occurs in the context of the society.

A covenant between teacher and learner is an enabling as-

Figure 2.1. Teaching/Learning Covenants

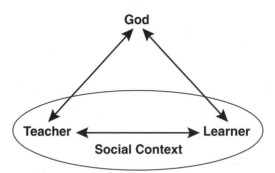

pect of the relationship. It is derived from the examples of relationships that we see in the theological interpretations of biblical covenant relationships.

The important educational elements of these relationships include commitment, conditions, vocation, responsibilities, respect, benefits, and sanctions. Covenants should be seen as *enabling*. They should have a social base and the ability to evolve according to the needs of parties.

The most important aspect of any teaching/learning covenant relationship is the "context," which involves other covenants. We cannot function as educators if we ignore or disregard the covenants that exist between God and the learner and between the learner and others in society.

An essential element in effective learning covenant relationships is respect for the covenant in which we engage with the learner as well as for the parallel covenant between God and the learner. We must recognize the existence of the other covenant and do everything possible to enhance it when we work with the learner.

If we wish to participate as teachers in Christian religious education, we need to consider the theological aspects that are relevant to our work. The lessons that we learn from the concept of the covenant will enable us to forge more effective relationships with learners.

TEACHING/LEARNING PRINCIPLES UNDERLYING THE LEARNING COVENANT AS A WHOLE

There are five principles that are critical to our understanding of the way in which the learning covenant actually works in the learning situation: (1) The adult is an independent, self-directed learner; (2) The adult is capable of identifying needs and interests for learning; (3) The adult is capable of planning a process for learning; (4) The adult is capable of conducting the learning process; (5) The adult can bring closure and evaluate the learning; and (6) The educator is a facilitator of the learning process, Adult educators in many countries have implemented the learning covenant model through reliance on adults' ability. These principles are drawn from the literature of adult education and the theological framework for this model.

The first principle, that the adult is an independent, self-directed learner, accepts the adult as an independently functioning person in the context of society who is able to make responsible, effective decisions.

Cyril Houle and Allen Tough provided the theoretical base

for an understanding of self-directed learning. Research by many colleagues, including Roger Hiemstra, Lucy Gugliemino, Pat Penland, and others, has confirmed the ability of learners to engage in self-directed learning activities. The review of many individual learning contracts or covenants by Malcolm Knowles, Rosemary Caffarella, Judith O'Donnell, and numerous other practitioners lends further credence to the research findings.

Adult educators in many countries have implemented the learning covenant model and adults' ability to function independently and responsibly has been demonstrated quite frequently. Malcolm Knowles and other authors have described its successful usage time after time in the literature of adult education.

The second principle, that the adult is capable of identifying needs and interests for learning, means that adults can and will identify specific aspects of their situation in order to proceed effectively with the learning process. There are times when the religious educator can assist in the learning process in order to make it more effective; nonetheless, the learner's ability to achieve the result is central to the process. Both practitioner reviews of complete contracts or covenants and research by Tough and numerous others confirm this fact.

The basis of the covenant is the learner's ability to develop a sense of awareness of his or her requirements for learning. Adult educators have attempted for some years, particularly since the 1960s, to involve learners in the process of "need identification." The educational theory and practice known as andragogy, which involves a process espoused by many educators of adults, incorporates learners into the process by asking them to share their needs and interests with the educator and other learners.

The success of the andragogical model and other models that incorporate the learner's identification of needs, interests, and requirements into the planning process testifies to the effectiveness of learners' contributions to the value of this approach. The growth of adult education in institutions and areas in which this model is used is considerable.

This principle of needs and interest identification is central to the issue of the learner's full participation in the covenant process. If learners are unable to fulfil their responsibilities in this part of the process, it is unlikely that they will do so in other parts of the process. The clear identification of needs and interests is critical to the success of the learning and enables the learner to avoid the difficulties associated with inappropriate choices and decisions.

The third principle, that the adult is capable of planning a process for learning, is important because religious educators frequently do not give adults sufficient opportunity to participate in the planning of learning. This principle implies that the adult can perform the tasks associated with planning, identifying the needs and interests and the specific areas to be learned, the resources to be used, the process of interaction with those resources, and the determination of basic criteria by which completion and success or failure are to be judged.

Guglielmino and others have identified characteristics that are relevant to the adult's abilities to perform such tasks. Her testing of students confirms the presence of such abilities.

This principle does not preclude the possibility of support from the religious educator in the learning process. Many learners do welcome support from those who offer to assist provided the support does not dominate the process of planning and preclude their interests.

In fact, many learners have developed successful learning covenants and contracts in a wide variety of settings over the years, as my own experience, as well as that of a number of other educators, attests.

Engagement in the planning of learning provides the learner with a significant sense of involvement at the very first stage of the learning activity. It is through this initial involvement that the learner begins to take ownership of the learning experience. The commitment to writing is a valuable part of the process of taking ownership.

The fourth principle, that the adult is capable of conducting the learning process, means adults can and do learn many things on a regular basis. It is the ability to learn that is central to this principle. Adults can interact with resources in a process that enables them to acquire new knowledge, skills, and attitudes.

Research by Allen Tough and his colleagues has been supplemented by the practical review of learning by Knowles and his colleagues to provide a picture of the important learning activities of adults using contracts or covenants. We know that many adults can learn successfully when the learning is focused on an issue of importance to them. Malcolm Knowles provides ample evidence of the capabilities of adults and the results of successful learning contracts in his books *Self-Directed Learning: A Guide for Learners and Teachers* and *Using Learning Contracts*.

The adult is able to function in many different areas of life, and learning is no exception. Religious educators can assist in the process, but they should not try to assume control or dominate the learning process.

The fifth principle, that the adult can bring closure and evaluate learning, refers to the adult's ability to determine when his or her learning requirements have been satisfied. The adult may need assistance in this process, but the essential point is that the adult must feel that the learning has reached a conclusion.

Who other than the learner can determine when the learner's needs have been met? There may be some who have opinions (that are informed or otherwise), but the adult learner's views must be considered on the matter.

If adults have responsibility for other aspects of their learning, it is not reasonable to suggest that they be excluded from the process of bringing closure to the learning. This principle completes the process of learning from the initial plan to the final decision to cease activities.

The sixth principle is that the educator is a facilitator of the learning process. The role of the religious educator is to support and "facilitate" the learning process to be a guide who shows the way and provides appropriate support at the moments when support is needed. The facilitator does not in any way dominate the process of learning. It is not a facilitator's role to provide all needed substantive content or to control every step in the process.

A relatively small percentage of adults participate in formal courses based upon traditional educational principles. The work of Allen Tough and others tells us that a much larger percentage of adults engage in significant amounts of learning on a regular basis. This so-called informal learning is often related to the job or occupation of the person or a dimension of life such as personal growth or leisure activities.

The religious education facilitator is able to enhance the learning that occurs for those adults who prefer not to participate in the so-called "formal" classroom, which is characterized by a predetermined content and a dominant teacher. This learning enhancement involves assistance to the adult learner in identifying what content is to be learned, what resources are to be used, how content is to be learned, and how closure is to be brought to the process of learning.

It is critical that the religious educator not violate the principles that have been elaborated in this chapter. The role of the facilitator assumes that these principles will be upheld and that the educator will be able to function effectively in relation to the adult learner.

THE THEORY UNDERLYING THIS
PROCEDURE AS A WHOLE

The theoretical base that was described earlier in this chapter has its roots in the work of Cyril Houle and Allen Tough. These authors described the learning process from a learner's perspective with an emphasis on the learner's abilities, skills, and content orientation.

Subsequent research focused on what came to be known as self-directed learning. The concept of self-direction came from the research findings of Tough and his colleagues in relation to the role of the learner as the main planner for learning projects.

Over time, the concept of self-directed learning was broadened to include other aspects of the learner's activities.

A large number of researchers began to investigate the phenomenon of self-directed learning in the general population and in specific groups within society. Rosemary Caffarella and Judith O'Donnell have described the research in a chapter in Huey Long's book on self-directed learning. It includes references to studies by Tough, Penland, Johns, Hiemstra, Morris, Rymell, and others.

Caffarella and O'Donnell correctly state that studies have reached the stage in which verification is no longer required. Further studies need only investigate a particular group or develop a new dimension of the research.

MORE RESOURCES TO HELP YOU FOLLOW UP WHAT YOU HAVE LEARNED IN THIS CHAPTER

1. Malcolm S. Knowles, *Using Learning Contracts: Practical Approaches to Individualizing and Structuring Learning* (San Francisco: Jossey-Bass, 1986), chaps. 1–2.

This book provides general background information about the nature of contracts.

2. Allen Tough, *The Adult's Learning Projects: A Fresh Approach to Theory and Practice in Adult Learning*, 2d ed. (Toronto: Ontario Institute for Studies in Education, 1979).

This book describes Tough's theory of self-directed learning. It changed educators' attitudes toward learning that occurs outside the classroom.

3. R. E. Y. Wickett, "Teaching and Learning in the Context of the Biblical Covenant," *Panorama: International Journal of Comparative Religious Education and Values.* 7, No.1 (1995): 65–71.

This article provides background on the theological impact of biblical covenants on the teaching-learning interaction.

4. Huey B. Long et al. eds., *Self-Directed Learning: Application and Theory* (Athens Adult Education Department, University of Georgia, 1988).

This book contains useful overviews of the relevant research by authors noted in this chapter.

5. R. E. Y. Wickett, *Models of Adult Religious Education Practice* (Birmingham, Ala. Religious Education Press, 1991), chap. 13.

This chapter provides an overview and a summary of the learning process.

3

PREPARING TO ENGAGE IN A LEARNING COVENANT

This chapter describes the various ways in which adult learners can begin the work that is necessary to achieve a successful learning experience using the covenant model. We know that many learners have not had the opportunity to use the covenant model in spite of its widespread use in certain educational institutions. This lack of prior learner involvement makes some form of preparation essential for those who have no prior experience of the model. This chapter emphasizes activities that are relevant to the learner who is using the covenant model for the first time, as well as commenting on the needs of learners who have used the model previously.

It is important to remember that many learners will be moving from a pattern of other directed learning, in which they play a passive role, to a pattern in which they will have an active role to play in determining the direction of their learning. This means that the preparatory process should familiarize them with the new process and assure them that they can engage successfully in a learning covenant.

Both the work that the learner does prior to the first meeting and the subsequent interaction that occurs during the first covenant meeting must reinforce this important dimension of the model. The process begins with the first contact between learner and facilitator.

There are two parts to the preparatory process. The first

part involves work done prior to any organized or formal meeting between the learner and the facilitator. The second part involves the first meeting between the learner and the facilitator.

Some learners may not feel comfortable in this process without a preliminary meeting with the facilitator. An alternative process may be offered to those who cannot use the two elements of advanced reading followed by personal meetings.

Malcolm Knowles has set the climate very effectively for learner participation in his first book on the topic of learning contracts, *Self-Directed Learning*. An effective introduction to the model can be arranged through the learner's reading of the first part of this book. Knowles himself confirms this use of the first book in his second book, *Using Learning Contracts*.

A personal meeting is essential at the early stage of the process in order to establish a good climate and a working relationship between the learner and the facilitator. This meeting can be made particularly productive through good preparation for the process for the learning covenant process.

I suggest that the following arrangements be made with learners who have either no experience or very limited experience with the learning covenant model. The latter group would include those who might have done some reading about this model but have no actual experience with the process. The suggested process is as follows:

I. Arrangements made prior to the first meeting
    a. Advance reading on the nature of the model should be assigned to the learner.
    b. The learner should be asked to consider his or her

ability to engage in this model. Does it seem appropriate as a model for learning?

c. The learner should be asked to identify and consider any issues relevant to the content area for potential learning for discussion at the first meeting.

II. Arrangements for the first meeting made between the learner and the facilitator

a. The relationship between learner and facilitator should be established. This is part of the learning climate.

b. All concerns about the learning covenant concept should be discussed as required.

c. All concerns about the specific process for the individual learning covenant should be discussed as required.

d. The learner's specific interests in relation to the content area to be learned should be identified and discussed.

e. Any institutional requirements should be discussed at this meeting to ensure that the learner understands any external factors that may have an impact on the learning process. Any external requirements that involve the evaluation process should be known by the learner in advance.

f. The specific nature of the learning contract that will be prepared by the learner should be identified. An example of a contract may be useful here. Knowles and other authors provide useful examples if no other examples are available.

g. Any possible resources or places to seek resources may be identified to encourage the learner and to assist her or him to begin the process of contract formation.

h. The learner should leave the meeting with the intention of returning to a second meeting with a first draft of the proposed learning covenant.

Learners who have previously completed a learning covenant in a successful fashion with the same facilitator may wish to proceed directly to the covenant formation stage. Specific learner interests (item II–D) , institutional requirements (item II–E), and resources (item II–G) should be discussed at the first meeting in this preliminary stage of the process.

Learners with prior learning covenant experience with a different facilitator will need to establish a relationship with the new facilitator. This process of building the relationship will ensure the proper climate for the learning process and will help to avoid any misunderstandings.

Other learners who are uncomfortable with the process and wish to have a face-to-face meeting with the facilitator should be encouraged to do so prior to undertaking further activities. This meeting should explain the basic nature of learning covenants, the process of covenant formation, and any specific questions that the learner may wish to ask.

PRIOR TO THE FIRST MEETING

Some learners may wish to understand the theological basis of the learning covenant concept. The readings that may be shared with the learner in advance of the first meeting might include one or more of the following works; the section on covenants in the *Interpreter's Dictionary of the Bible*, Wickett's chapter on "contract learning and the covenant" in

Theological Interpretations and Adult Education or his article "Teaching and Learning in the Context of the Biblical Covenant" in *Panorama: International Journal of Comparative Religious Education and Values*, or the relevant sections of a good biblical commentary. Other learners may be content with a summary discussion of the nature of biblical covenants.

Additional useful reading should focus on the nature of the covenant. Part 1 (p.7–28) of Knowles's book *Self-Directed Learning: A Guide for Learners and Teachers* provides a good introduction. The chapter that describes the covenant model in *Models of Adult Religious Education Practice* may provide additional information for some advanced learners. Judith O'Donnell and Rosemary Caffarella's chapter on learning contracts in Michael Galbraith's book *Adult Learning Methods* will also be of value to some learners.

After the learners have reviewed the appropriate literature, they should be asked to think about their interests and needs for learning. This can be a useful exercise for those who have not read these writings on covenants, although some learners may have done considerable reading of the literature prior to their involvement with the facilitator.

The learner should then be invited to attend a session with the facilitator to discuss any concerns and outstanding issues. Any concerns the learner has about the covenant model should be brought to the intial meeting with the facilitator.

THE FIRST MEETING BETWEEN LEARNER
AND FACILITATOR

This is the first and crucial step in the process toward a learning covenant. The relationship between the learner and the facilitator must be established, and the learner must leave the meeting with positive feelings toward the facilitator and the covenant process. Positive feelings are assured if the learner anticipates a successful learning experience.

Malcolm Knowles describes climate settings as a critical issue in his book *The Modern Practice of Adult Education: From Pedagogy to Andragogy*. The first session with a learner should ensure that the appropriate climate for the learning process is established. Two pivotal dimensions of climate setting are interpersonal concerns and content. The interpersonal dimension involves the working relationship between the learner and the facilitator, whereas the content dimension provides both the learner and the facilitator with a sense of direction and confidence that the learning can be achieved.

Interpersonal relationships are central to success in everyday life similarly, the learning covenant requires effective working relationships between the learner and the facilitator in order to achieve success.

It is also possible to engage in learning covenants in a group situation. The learning group may provide an opportunity to develop relationships with other learners who have similar interests. A combination of good relationships with the other learners and the facilitator can be very valuable.

The first meeting of a group of learners who wish to engage in the covenant process will provide time for building relationships, for example, through the mutual sharing of information, particularly of interests in content areas for the covenant.

If possible, specific samples of draft and completed learning covenants should be shown to the learner at this first meeting. The facilitator should identify some human and material resources and their locations (e.g., libraries or other organizations) at this time in order to encourage the learner. This will enable the learner to begin to investigate the resources and their location as the preparation of the first draft of the covenant begins and to have confidence in the availability of resources for learning.

The next phase of the process is to assure the learner that successful learning can occur through the application of this model and that the desired content can be obtained through the suggested process of the learning covenant.

The learner needs to feel confident about her ability to produce a draft covenant for the next meeting. There are two factors that contribute to this requisite feeling of assurance. The facilitator's knowledge of both the potential resource base for content and the process for interaction with the resources will help to assure the learner, since, the facilitator knows what is available and how to use it.

If the covenant is to be used for specific training purposes, certification, or for academic credit, it is important to identify any requirements that an institution may have. For example, the learning may be aimed at preparing for a specific function of lay ministry. You may explore together the ministry that is to be performed and what expectations the faith community has of the person who performs it. This discussion has the additional value of placing the learning in its appropriate context.

The facilitator should describe the nature of the specific components of the learning covenant during the first meeting. The learner should be clear about the nature of each component and the items that are to be included to make the covenant workable.

It is important that the learner knows what she is to do to prepare for the next meeting. Chapter 5 of this book describes the various dimensions of the learning covenant in some detail. Malcolm Knowles, as well as Judith O'Donnell and Rosemary Cafarella, have provided examples of general contracts that can be used with learners. The examples provided in chapters 9–11 of this book focus on the area of learning covenants for religious content and may be used with learners as well.

Adult religious educators who use this model over a period of time should collect copies of covenants and evidence that supports their successful completion. My students who have not used the learning covenant model before find these examples to be of great value. These students often use these examples as "templates" for their own learning covenants.

If the facilitator of the covenant has any doubts about the learner's ability to complete the covenant or about the suitability of the content to the learning covenant model, this is the time to address the issue. Consider the following questions:

a. Does the learner have the ability to identify specific areas of content and to prepare and conduct a covenant?

b. Does the content fit the learning covenant model? Content that is less specific and more exploratory may be more appropriate for another model.

c. Is the religious educator prepared to assume the facilitative role? This means that the religious educator is prepared to work cooperatively with the learner during both the decision-making process and the implementation phase.

A lack of confidence about any of these issues should lead the religious educator to reconsider proceeding with the use of the learning covenant model.

SUMMARY

The following points are essential to the process of preparation to engage in the learning covenant process:

1. Help the learner to move from being other-directed to being self-directed.

2. Provide the learner with an adequate understanding of the learning covenant model through appropriate readings or a personal explantion.

3. Help the learner consider what content is to be learned in its context.

4. Provide the learner with information about potential resources and the various resource bases that will be relevant.

5. Provide the learner with information that will enable the writing of a draft covenant.

6. And most important of all: Establish a good working relationship with the learner.

MORE RESOURCES TO HELP YOU FOLLOW UP WHAT YOU HAVE LEARNED FROM THIS CHAPTER:

1. Malcolm S. Knowles, *The Modern Practice of Adult Education: From Pedagogy to Andragogy*, rev. and updated (Chicago: Follett, 1980), 223–226.

2. R. E. Y. Wickett, *Models of Adult Religious Education Practice* (Birmingham, Alab.: Religious Education Press, 1991), 59–61.

If you wish to learn more about climate setting, it is reviewed in detail in Knowles's book. Both books provide general assistance in setting the appropriate learning climate.

3. J. Diero, *Alternative Learning Experiences: A Handbook for Contract Learning* (U.S. Department of Education, Educational Resources Information Clearinghouse, 1980), 7–23.

This article provides a good introduction to the basic concepts of learning covenants in a short time.

4. Hedley G. Dimmock, *Groups: Leadership and Group Development,* rev. ed. (San Diego, Calif.: University Associates, 1983).

This book is an excellent resource for more information about the ways in which groups function and the ways in which they can be helped to work effectively.

5. Allen Tough, Virginia Griffin, Bill Barnard, and Donald Brundage, *The Design of Self-Directed Learning,* ed. Reg Her-

man (Toronto: Department of Adult Education, Ontario Institute for Studies in Education, and Ryerson Polytechnical Institute, 1980). This is a package of print and videotaped materials. Review the videotape component with Bill Barnard as the experienced facilitator who is in conversation with Lew Lewis, the learner. This tape demonstrates a working discussion on the issue of covenant formation.

4

IDENTIFYING RESOURCES FOR THE LEARNING COVENANT

Virtually every type of learning activity uses external resources as sources for content. This is also true for all learning covenants. External resources include any human or material resource with the exception of the individual learner's internal personal resources, such as memory. The identification of the appropriate resources for any learning covenant is a central activity for both the learner and the facilitator.

The learner also benefits from developing skills in identifying resources for learning. As the facilitator is involved in every learning activity, skills that the learner acquires in identifying and acquiring of appropriate resources will be most helpful in any future self-directed learning activity.

The learner's tasks are to locate resources and to determine the process for the use of the various resources that have been selected. These tasks take both time and effort. They occur at the earliest stages of covenant formation and may be necessary at other stages in the process.

The facilitator's task is to ensure that the learner is able to find the appropriate resources to incorporate into the covenant. This is one of the few aspects of a learning covenant in which the facilitator makes direct statements instead of asking questions. These statements may identify specific resources and their locations or they may simply indicate the location of a resource base such as a special library. Suggesting a resource base location may encourage the learner to search for resources and to develop skills that will be useful in future learning activities.

Knowles emphasizes the decisions about learning strategies, thereby giving learning strategies more importance than the location and acquisition of resources. It is my view that first-time covenant learners will benefit in particular from an effective search for resources that are first located and then placed within a "strategy," process, or plan.

When the facilitator advises the learner, it is important to remember that suggested resources need to be suitable and accessible, as well as fit into the learning process or plan. The suitability of the resource is dependent upon the learner's ability to make use of it for the intended religious education purpose. Accessibility means that the learner can obtain the resource for its required use.

The resources available in many communities are quite substantial. Libraries with extensive materials may be located in a local faith community as well as in the larger civic community. The materials may then be identified in the learning covenant. But these libraries are obvious locations. Local experts are often willing to contribute their time and talents to assist the individual learner. Computer-accessible resource bases allow the learner to move well beyond the local context into The World Wide Web.

THE NATURE OF THE RESOURCES

Various resources are available to assist the learner. These resources include both the human and the material resources with which the learner will interact during the process of the learning covenant. The following sections describe some of the many human and material resources that may be included in learning covenants and the factors that determine their inclusion in the final draft of the learning covenant.

Human Resources

Human resources that have been used for learning covenants include both substantive content specialists and the peer resources who are often involved in learning activities. It is the role of the facilitator to enable the process, but both "experts" (or substantive content specialists) and "peer" resources can be used to support the acquisition of new content.

One advantage that the learning covenant has over the models with a total or major classroom commitment is the learner's ability to meet resource persons outside of the immediate institutional setting. The learner can make contact with persons who have special knowledge or skills that the learner can use effectively to augment material resources.

If the learner wishes to explore an area in which the facilitator has limited expertise, another knowledgeable person may be found to supply the necessary new knowledge or skill. There are many situations in which the best source of content is a different person. Religious educators should not be concerned about the involvement of external resource persons. These resource persons do not displace the facilitator. The facilitator's primary responsibility is overall coordination of the learning process in cooperation with the learner. The expert resource person, when used effectively, simply adds to the process.

Some learning covenants put the learner at a distance from the institution and from the covenant facilitator for periods of time. Resource persons who are available at the distant location can be identified and engaged in the learning process. Thus the learner can make effective use of the resource person and hence more effective use of time spent in an alternate location.

Some learners find it psychologically difficult to approach an "expert". Perhaps they have limited social experience with people who are described as experts. Extra assistance and encouragement may be required to convince these learners to make the contacts that will enable them to proceed with the next step of covenant formation.

My own experience, with external resource persons as well as the experience of many learners, has been very positive. Religious educators should be thankful for the efforts of those who often contribute with no sense of recompense for their work with learners.

Persons who are not considered experts but have relevant experience or background to the content to be learned can also make a positive contribution. These people are often referred to as "peer resources". They may be friends or acquaintances whose sharing of their own experience will be of value in the learning process.

Peer resources are particularly helpful when the learning covenant is part of a group learning situation. Learners discover their common interests and may be encouraged to work in co-operation. The group may be organized into a series of learning partnerships in order to take advantage of common interests. They may share information gathered from other resources and encourage each other throughout the process.

The religious educator may use peer resources when there is a person with slightly more experience than the learner. A person who is engaged in a particular form of ministry may not have enough background to be considered an expert but may have experience that is of value when shared with another person who is engaged in a learning process.

Many religious educators are accustomed to being the sole person to interact with the learner. When other persons are introduced to the learning process in other models, it is often within the safe, controlled confines of the classroom. The learning covenant model encourages the learner to become involved with as many external human resources as appropriate. The impact of this process of sharing is that the educator *must* become the facilitator in order to assist the learner to maximize the value of external contacts.

Material Resources

Material resources include all nonhuman resources that may be used by the learner. It includes both print, visual, and electronic resources for learning. These potential resources are often very extensive, but the learner may need some assistance in identifying, locating, and obtaining the resources required for a particular learning covenant.

Some learners may not be familiar with the various locations of resources for learning in their community and beyond. The facilitator must help them locate and use the facilities that are required to obtain resources for the covenant.

Print resources are considered most useful by persons who have spent most of their lives using the print medium. No one can doubt their value to many learners. It is important to remember that there are some learners whose literacy skills are quite limited. These people would benefit from access to other resources or to print materials at their reading level.

Such issues as the learner's reading level and interest in reading should determine the balance and nature of reading materials for the covenant. If the learner *likes* to read, print materials can be most useful. Other learners may wish to minimize the amount of reading in favor of either interpersonal interaction, such as an interview or discusssion, or video or audio materials, such as videotapes or audiotapes. Some learners may not read well or they may simply learn more effectively from nonprint material.

Busy adult learners need reasonable access to the print resources, but obtaining these materials through interlibrary loans or other means can be time-consuming. The religious educator should assist the learner to obtain everything as quickly and as easily as possible. It is advisable to focus on local resources and to turn to other places only as a last resort. Interlibrary loans may take some time, but they can be valuable.

Electronic materials are becoming a major factor among the material resources that adults use. There is a diversity of nonprint materials available today, including films, audio- and videotapes, videodiscs, and computer programs.

Many adults find visual images useful for learning. Films

and videotapes should be considered where they are relevant and accessible. They are not used for "teacher relief" or as an alternative form of stimulation. They are of value for their content, but they can be used to stimulate other learning activities also.

Many learners find videotapes of their own activities to be invaluable to skills acquisition, since they give people the opportunity to see themselves as others see them. This method is quite popular in large muscle motor skill development, but many religious educators have used it extensively in the areas of interpersonal skills such as pastoral counseling.

The age of the computer is now upon us. There are many ways in which the computer can improve access to resources. Vast amounts of information can be stored and retrieved very quickly. The learner may need considerable guidance in accessing this world, but the advantages will be considerable. Public libraries in many communities provide computer access to electronic networks, and other educational institutions such as universities often have excellent resources.

Computer-assisted instruction is possible where there is a prepackaged program for learning. A careful choice of the package, or a part of the package, is critical to this resource because it must be suited to the learner's needs for content and process.

The learner may choose to access the Internet. There are several resource bases containing religious material that can be accessed electronically via the computer.

There are electronic magazines, such as *Church bytes*, that provide more information about computer resources on religion and how to access them. A good publication by Ed Krol, which describes how these electronic systems work, is entitled *The Whole Internet: A User's Guide and Catalogue.* This is a general secular resource. A very useful resource in the area of religion is the *Electric Mystics' Guide to the Internet,* which is available via electronic mail. Both documents provide a good working knowledge of the electronic communication system. The *Electric Mystics' Guide* contains a directory of current electronic documents, online conferences, serials, software, and archives relevant to religious studies. This material is currently available via the Internet at LISTSERV@ACADVM1. UOTTAWA.CA or LISTSERV@UOTTAWA on Bitnet as MYSTICSV1–TXT AND MYSTICSV3–TXT.

Many newcomers to the use of these electronic media struggle to learn to identify the various electronic resource bases and to access them. Yet the technology is becoming easier to use and continues to provide access to a wide range of information.

THE SELECTION OF RESOURCES

This is an important part of learning covenant formation. Once resources have been located, a decision must be made about which ones to use. The criteria described in the following paragraphs can assist this process.

The learner's ability to make use of a resource is a critically important issue to be decided. If the learner has the background necessary to use the resource, it can be considered for the covenant. This background may include prior learning experience and the requisite level of reading skills.

Given the learner's ability to use the resource, the next most important issue is the appropriateness of the content of the resource. Does the resource contain substantive content that the learner requires? If the answer to this question is affirmative, the resource should be included in the draft list of resources.

Before including a resource in the final list of the covenant, the issue of appropriateness, or "fit," into the learning process should be addressed. Does the resource fit into the process of the learning covenant or not? Duplication should be avoided where possible, but it may be useful to have a backup resource should the primary resource become unavailable.

The resources must also be accessible to the learner during the learning process. If resource people or materials are unavailable for any reason during the particular time frame of the covenant or if the resource materials are not located in reasonable proximity, the learner may not wish to include them in the covenant.

Resources that (1) provide specific substantive content, (2) are accessible and usable, and (3) fit the plan that the learner wishes to follow should be included in the final version of the learning covenant. The issue of sequencing the use of resources will be discussed in the next chapter. The learner should be able to proceed most comfortably when all this has occurred.

SUMMARY

The following points summarize the most important issues of resource location and selection:

1. Assist the learner to locate appropriate resources through the identification of both specific resources and resource bases such as libraries and so on.

2. Advise on the potential use of a wide range of human and material resources.

3. Help the learner to identify appropriate human resources, which may include both outside experts and peers.

4. Help the learner to identify material resources that include a wide variety of electronic options such as audio- and videotapes, interactive videodiscs, and computers.

5. Assist the learner to consider the ways in which the resources fit productively into the learning process.

Religious educators would do well to remember that the learner can increase independent learning skills through a better understanding of where and how to locate external resources. The process of resource identification can be used in future learning activities when the facilitator is not available or required.

MORE RESOURCES TO HELP YOU FOLLOW UP WHAT YOU HAVE LEARNED FROM THIS CHAPER:

1. Judith M. O'Donnell and Rosemary S. Caffarella, "Learning Contracts," in *Adult Learning Methods: A Guide for Effective Instruction*, ed. Michael W. Galbraith (Malabar, Fla.: Krieger, 1990), 154–55.

A comprehensive list of the various types of resources can be found here.

2. R. E. Y. Wickett and Mary Freitag, "Resources for Adult Religious Education," in *Adult Religious Education: A Journey of Faith*, ed. Marie S. Gillen and Maurice Taylor (Birmingham, Ala.: Religious Education Press, 1994).

This chapter describes the many resources that are of value to the adult learner.

3. Joan Robertson, Sharon Saberton, and Virginia Griffin, *Learning Partnerships: Interdependent Learning in Adult Education* (Toronto: Ontario Institute for Studies in Education, Department of Adult Education, 1985).

This is an excellent source for information about peer learning.

4. Ed Krol, *The Whole Internet: A User's Guide and Catalogue* (Sebastopol, Calif.: O'Reilly, 1992).

This is the most current resource for information about the major electronic communication system, the Internet.

5. Malcolm S. Knowles, *Using Learning Contracts: Approaches to Individualizing and Structuring Learning* (San Francisco, Jossey-Bass, 1986).

Knowles shows the wide range of possible resources in the many contracts that are used to illustrate his ideas in this book.

5

DRAFTING THE
LEARNING COVENANT

Because learners often have strong feelings of ownership for their covenant, it is important that they participate fully in the process of producing the draft covenant. This participation extends to the decision to produce the document.

Many authors of adult education works in this area, including Malcolm Knowles and Judith O'Donnell and Rosemary Caffarella, have indicated the necessity of making the learner *the* central party to the writing of the learning contract or covenant. The process of writing makes the learner consider the covenant more carefully and provides a basis for the facilitator's reactions.

The other important aspect of writing the covenant is the sense of ownership of the learning that emerges from the learner's commitment to his or her work on the printed page. This commitment may be the most valuable result of the process. Facilitators and other religious educators try to obtain the learner's commitment to the learning process in virtually every model they use. There are very few successful contract or covenant situations without serious commitment on the part of the learner to the learning process.

One confirmation of a high level of learner commitment is the problem that is seen in many draft versions of learning covenants. Learners often want to include too much. A major task for the religious education facilitator is to ensure that the learning covenant is appropriate in terms of the learner's capabilities, including time, effort, and interests.

PROCESS FOR COVENANT FORMATION

The following process should be followed with first time learners:

a. Ensure that the learner develops a clear focus for the learning.

b. Ensure that the learner has adequate knowledge of available resources to begin the process.

c. Ensure that the learner understands the format and the various components to be included in the learning covenant.

d. Request the learner to commit ideas in writing based upon the format for a learning covenant.

e. Review the contents of the draft learning covenant with the learner to ensure an adequate level of understanding of the implications of the document that is being proposed.

f. Request the learner to revise the proposed learning covenant to include all items on which there is mutual agreement and return to the next meeting with a revised document ready for acceptance and implementation.

All these factors are important in the formation of the learning covenant. Learners with prior learning contract or covenant experience will proceed quickly through most parts of this process. This issue is taken up later in the chapter.

Learning covenants require the learner to have a clear focus for the learning. Other educational models, such as the andragogical model or independent study model, are more effective in support of exploratory learning. The learner should engage the content in a discussion in order to achieve a sense of clarity about the focus of the learning activities.

As described in chapter 4, certain information has been gathered about resources as part of the process of covenant formation. The search for additional resources should continue until the final draft of the covenant is submitted for approval or until learner and facilitator are confident that they have identified all that are needed.

Questions to Be Asked about the Learning Covenant

The components of the learning covenant may be identified and clarified for the learner through the use of specific questions. The following questions illustrate possible questions that may be asked:

a. What is it about?
    What are the objectives?

b. What will you need to learn this?
    What resources will you use?
    How will you use these resources?
    What are your learning resources and strategies?

c. Do you have dates for completion of certain activities?
    What are your target dates?
    What is your timetable?

d. When will you know that you have completed what you
   set out to do?
   How will you know that you have really learned something?

e. What evidence of accomplishment will you require?
   How will you evaluate the learning?

The first question of each set is for those who are unfamiliar
with or wish to avoid educational terms. The second question
of each set is for learners who are familiar and comfortable
with educational terms.

It is important to use the correct approach for each type of
learner. Some learners are intimidated by the use of educational jargon, whereas others may be helped through the use
of technical terms that they understand fully.

These questions provide religious educators with the components of the learning covenant, goals and objectives, resources and procedures, timetable, evidence of accomplishment, and criteria for evaluation. Each component should be
included in some form in every learning covenant.

The first stage of formation for many learning covenants is
writing down the information. This written component enables the facilitator to respond to very specific items and to
see the overall nature of the covenant. It is also helpful for
most learners to engage in the process of writing their ideas in
a learning covenant format.

Some learners like the visual effect that occurs through the
visual display of the proposed learning process. Other learners
prefer to write in paragraphs and to use words alone to state
their process. A visual effect can be created by using the

following headings at the top of the page and inserting the text in the appropriate columns.

Figure 5.1 Headings for Learning Covenants

Objectives	Learning strategies and resources	Evidence of accomplishment learning	Evaluation of the	Time table

If the draft of the covenant is to be written in paragraph form, the specific nature of the document will depend upon the learning situation. The objectives should be stated in at least one paragraph. The learning strategies and resources should be integrated with the time schedule into a series of paragraphs with an activity from the strategy as the central focus. The details of resources and the timetable or schedule should be incorporated into each paragraph. An alternate approach may be chosen if the nature of the learning covenant requires it.

Specific examples of learning covenants may be found in this book in chapters 9–11. These chapters review learning covenants with persons training for ordained or lay ministry or with those wishing to learn for their own individual purposes in a content area related to an aspect of religion.

Chapter 7 describes the system of evaluation that is consistent with this educational model. Both the nature of evidence and the criteria for evaluation are described in detail. Specific examples, evidence, and criteria for evaluation are provided with the samples of written learning covenants.

One factor that is often overlooked is the timetable or schedule for learning activities. If the learner is involved in other activities, such as other courses, employment, or personal commitments, the timetable should ensure that enough time is available for the learning tasks included in the covenant.

The religious education facilitator must ensure that the timetable is realistic. Many learners attempt to do too much in too short a period of time. The facilitator should suggest adequate time for each task and for integrative activities, including the evaluation. The process of monitoring should be related to the timetable and relevant learning activities.

The agreed times and dates for meetings between learner and religious education facilitator may be included in the final draft of the covenant, but they should be decided at that time. These arrangements will provide a guide for the monitoring process but should be flexible.

The learner who is working on the learning covenant apart from the facilitator, at home or at the office, must be able to contact the facilitator for the solution to any problem that arises during the writing phase. The facilitator should provide the learner with reasonable access via the telephone or in person for as long as the learner is working on the activities of the covenant. Many learners work on their tasks at times that may seem strange to us as facilitators!

Working with the First-Time Covenant Learner

The learner may feel anxious about the development and implementation of a learning covenant. Everything possible should be done to help the learner relax during the process of covenant formation.

The vast majority of those participating in a learning covenant for the first time have little idea about how this model works. Most learners are accustomed to teacher-directed learning processes that tell them what to do and how to do it. They must be helped to take responsibility for their work.

The most successful covenants result from the learner's commitment and sense of responsibility. The religious education facilitator should do everything possible during this phase of covenant formation to ensure that the learner feels supported and is able to take responsibility.

A mixture of questions and statements, with an emphasis on the questions, assist the learner to develop a sense of control. The process of dialogue begins effectively with a question, and the learner feels the inclusive nature of the discussion. As the learner's answers and other comments are given value by the facilitator in the dialogue, the learner begins to experience a sense of partnership with the facilitator. A sense of ownership grows from this type of discussion.

It is also important to provide the learner with options by showing sample covenants that others have used. The intention is to have the learner create a covenant that reflects his situation, not to reproduce someone else's covenant with a few changes in words. The facilitator may decide that a particular format for the covenant is appropriate for a particular type of learner, but several examples of the same format may still be shared.

Working with Low Literary Learners

The religious education facilitator who is working with a learner with a low literacy level may take an alternate approach to the creation of a formal learning covenant. A very simple written covenant may be undertaken with direct support in order to assist the learner to increase her literacy level. A verbal covenant that is known and clearly understood by both parties should also be quite acceptable.

If the facilitator has literacy training, the simple learning covenant may prove to be the best approach. The complications of literacy training and the learning covenant may prove very difficult for some learners and facilitators.

The learning covenant procedure can be used to help the learner improve his reading and writing skills as part of the overall process of becoming better educated. This involves the writing aspect and not prior preparation through reading, unless some learning contract or covenant with very low reading levels is available for review. The experts who have written about this model have done so at a level that is not understood easily by those with less than a high school education.

A simple draft covenant should be drawn up by the learner and the religious education facilitator together. The flow chart in figure 5.2, which is similar to figure 5.1, might be used with the simplification of the headings.

The section under the heading "How will I learn it?" includes both resources and strategies.

The learner can be helped to read the headings, if necessary, and the learner and the religious education facilitator can complete the statements underneath each heading using the

Figure 5.2 Headings for a Simple Learning
Covenant

What am I going to learn?	How will I learn it? With what?	How will I know when I am done?	Dates

appropriate language level. Reading and writing skills can be incorporated into the process using this approach.

Working with the Experienced Covenant Learner

This can be a very pleasurable and productive experience because the learner knows what can be accomplished and is prepared to develop a covenant that can be successful. Although the learner understands the process of developing learning covenants, she may need to explore the substantive content area of the learning covenant carefully in order to achieve a desirable result.

New substantive content requires new resources and new strategies, including time schedules. It also suggests the need for new forms of evidence and new criteria for evaluation. The learner's familiarity with the process should not inhibit the full exploration of the relevant content issues.

The religious education facilitator may use questions effectively to clarify the learning covenant with experienced covenant learners and can make statements with less concern about the development of self-direction. Most learners who are experienced in the learning covenant model have made the transition to self-direction with the successful completion of a previous learning covenant. It is important to respect this transition and its ramifications during subsequent covenants.

SUMMARY

The formation of an appropriately planned learning covenant is critical to the overall process. This chapter has described the key issues in the development of the written form of the covenant that the learner and the facilitator can use to guide the learning process and to govern the interaction with the learner. The following points are intended to guide the religious education facilitator in helping the learner through the process of covenant formation:

1. Assist the learner to become self-directed during the process of covenant formation.

2. Ensure that the learner has described a clear statement of purpose, adequate resources, and a strategy for learning with an appropriate timetable for the learning covenant.

3. Ensure that the learner has arranged for adequate evidence of accomplishment to satisfy both individual or institutional requirements if necessary.

4. Help first-time learners to become more comfortable and confident with the content and the process of the learning covenant model.

5. Ensure that experienced covenant learners focus on content and relevant strategies for learning.

These key points bring the learner to the stage of a well- conceived draft covenant, which will bring both facilitator and learner close to a final document. The next chapter reviews the procedure for acceptance of the covenant and its implementation.

MORE RESOURCES TO HELP YOUR FOLLOW UP WHAT YOU HAVE LEARNED FROM THIS CHAPTER:

The following materials contain copies of draft covenants that can be reviewed by the learner for more information about the contents of learning covenants:

1. J. Diero, *Alternative Learning Experiences: A Handbook for Contract Learning* (U.S. Department of Education, Educational Resources Information Clearinghouse, 1980), 7–18.

2. Malcolm S. Knowles, *Self-Directed Learning: A Guide for Learners and Teachers* (Chicago: Follett, 1975), 46–58.

3. Malcolm S. Knowles, *Using Learning Contracts: Practical Approaches to Individualizing and Structuring Learning* (San Francisco: Jossey-Bass, 1986), 33–36, 52–54, 132–139.

4. Judith M. O'Donnell and Rosemary S. Caffarella, "Learning Contracts," in *Adult Learning Methods: A Guide for Effective Instruction,* ed. Michael W. Galbraith (Malabar, Fla.: Krieger, 1990), 140–144, 150–153.

5. Allen M. Tough, *The Adult's Learning Projects: A Fresh Approach to Theory and Practice in Adult Learning,* 2d ed. (Toronto: Ontario Institute for Studies in Education, 1979).

This seminal work reviews the issues of self-direction.

6

ACCEPTING, IMPLEMENTING, AND MONITORING THE LEARNING COVENANT

The actual acquisition of substantive content begins effectively with the acceptance of the learning covenant by the learner and the religious education facilitator. After accepting the final copy of the covenant, both the learner and the facilitator are prepared to begin the actual learning process. The learner establishes a degree of independence after the covenant has been accepted, but the facilitator must continue to support the process of learning. This chapter describes the process of the learning covenant from its acceptance to the final evaluation process. This is the most important part of the process for most learners.

It is important to remember the clear role differences between the learner and the facilitator and between the facilitator and the resource person. These differences enable the learner to grow into a more competent self-directed learner through the effective use of resources during the learning process.

The new skills, that the learner will acquire through independent functioning, are also useful to the learner's longer-term learning activities. The religious education facilitator should provide the support that is required during the learning process for present learning as well as for long-term skill development.

ACCEPTING THE COVENANT

The learning covenant must be agreed by both parties before the learner can proceed. Previous drafts of the document have prepared both the learner and the facilitator for this stage in the process. This is clearly the most important stage in the process so far.

All aspects of the learning covenant should be described to the satisfaction of both parties. No confusion or uncertainty about purpose, substantive content, resources, process, and evaluation procedures should exist for either party. A final review of the document on a section by section basis should occur to ensure this state of certainty.

The religious education facilitator is responsible for the appropriateness and the success of the process for learning. At this time, she should request assurances from the learner that the resources identified by the learner are available and that any necessary institutional or community requirements are met.

If external requirements of any faith community or institution are to be met, particular attention should be paid to the evaluation process in order to ensure that both parties are clear about the requirements of the situation. This refers to both the evidence and the criteria for evaluation that are discussed in detail in chapter 7 of this book.

The religious education facilitator would do well to review the proposed monitoring process as part of the learning covenant. As chapter 5 suggests, the meetings between learner and facilitator should be clearly identified. These meetings may be scheduled in the final copy of the document. The facilitator should be available at a convenient location for all meetings, and the learner and facilitator should agree to a schedule of meetings.

This is the time to recognize the transition from planning to implementation. The learner should be congratulated in some manner for the achievement of the learning covenant. A few words of recognition and encouragement are most appropriate at this time. This is particularly true for learners who are using the learning covenant model for the first time.

The learner should provide the religious education facilitator with a copy of the document to which both parties agreed. The facilitator should keep this copy available for meetings and should record any agreed changes to the original learning covenant.

It should be stressed at this time that the document is not legalistic in nature. It is intended to guide the learning process and may be altered by necessity and mutual consent. The learner should remember that this is not a covenant of the Mosaic type, and should be willing to enter into the "spirit" of the covenant concept.

IMPLEMENTING AND MONITORING
THE LEARNING COVENANT

The learner is responsible for implementing the learning covenant, whereas the religious education facilitator is responsible for monitoring it. Understanding the distinction between these two functions will result in both being undertaken appropriately and efficiently.

Many covenants use the religious education facilitator as a resource person at times. When it is necessary and appropriate, the facilitator may assume the alternate role of resource person. The learner should recognize this resource role as a specific time is arranged in the schedule for this interaction between the learner and resource person. It also may be possible to combine the two roles at times when there are other external resource persons.

A special time slot that is separate from the arrangements for monitoring may be placed in the timetable with the other meetings with resource persons. Monitoring sessions should be conducted in a manner that is different from the process of "content transmission."

The two parties should proceed according to the arrangements that have been described and agreed. Adjustments to the process and schedule can and should be made at times. These adjustments should be discussed and agreed to by both parties as they become necessary.

The Implementation Process

Implementation is the sole responsibility of the learner. The learner begins the work, which has been approved by both parties. The process should continue under conditions that have been agreed by both parties. There is no need for outside interference from the religious education facilitator; however, the facilitator's support is often a necessary component for those who are experiencing the learning covenant model for the first time.

Learners experience many things as they discover the joys of independence. This discovery of independence will involve the development and use of new skills and the resultant satisfaction that is a part of this process.

The religious education facilitator must foster this independence in order to ensure the positive aspects of this experience. It will be a reflection on the facilitator's skills if these feelings of success and independence are not achieved.

A broad range of emotions may occur in the learner during the implementation process. Every religious educator knows the joys and frustrations that come during successful learning experiences. The key to success is to continue the process even though all does not go smoothly all the time. The learner should enjoy the successes and learn from the difficulties that arise during the process.

The Monitoring Process

This process enables the religious education facilitator to support the learner during the conduct of the learning. The monitoring process enables the learner to discuss, clarify, reflect, question, or reject all with the support of a person who is knowledgeable and supportive.

Most religious education facilitators find the experience of monitoring to be different from the experience of other teaching/learning situations, since the learner in the covenant model functions independently. The facilitator is not present at all times when the learner is learning, nor is she ever able to control the process as educators often do in the classroom.

If the learner is able to implement the covenant and learn through the use of this model, the facilitator does not need to be present at all times during the process. Feelings of uncertainty and discomfort with this part of the process merely reflect the conditioning produced by years of direct involvement in the classroom setting.

The essential aspect of monitoring is a series of meetings at intervals in the learning process. The learner should have acquired sufficient learning experiences before each meeting to produce a valuable exchange of thoughts and ideas.

The religious education facilitator should be able to intervene in a manner that enhances the learning process. This will involve helping the learner to discover the connections between various items of substantive content that have been acquired during the process as outlined in the learning covenant.

It may be very helpful to review the written document of the learning covenant prior to the learner's visits. Particular attention should be given to the specific activities that have been completed most recently and the ways in which they fit into the overall pattern of the learning process.

The meeting place should be one in which both parties feel comfortable and can discuss all matters easily. Any unnecessary distractions should be avoided in these meetings just as they are in classroom teaching. A neutral place, such as an office in which interruptions can be eliminated or minimized, is a good choice.

The learner and the religious education facilitator should have comfortable chairs located at the appropriate distance for friendly interchange. Chairs of roughly equal dimensions will emphasize the nature of the relationship between the two parties.

The facilitator should obtain any resources to be shared with the learner in advance of the session when they are required. Any resource that is relevant to the session should be kept available. If it is to be used at a later time, it may be kept on file and retrieved at the appropriate moment.

The religious educator should encourage the learner to locate and obtain resources whenever possible. Learner self-reliance will result from the learner's confidence in his own ability to perform this critical task in the learning process.

Inquiring about the state of the process at the beginning of a meeting may bring problems to light. This is always a good way to begin a session because it provides an opportunity for the learner and the facilitator to renew their relationship after a time apart.

A learner takes the initiative in the meeting because she has unanswered questions or problems. These items should be considered as soon as possible in the meeting. This type of discussion enables both the learner and the facilitator to avoid any distractions from unfinished items when they wish to focus on other agenda items.

If the learner seeks support and guidance from the facilitator, the learner's own outline should provide a sense of direction for both parties. A religious education facilitator can turn the focus back to the learner in a guided process whereby the learner and facilitator cooperate in order to solve a problem. This will discourage the learner from abdicating responsibility to the facilitator.

In most situations, the facilitator may find that questions are useful as a tool in discussions with the learner. A question may be used to open areas of thought or to focus the learner. It may lead in a new direction that the learner will want to follow. It may also lead to an immediate conclusion but no further activity in the area.

Good questioning techniques are a result of practice and a clear plan. The plan for the questioning process should focus on the learning process as outlined in the learning covenant. Ask questions about each important component of the learning covenant when each component is in process or recently completed.

The learner may having difficulties "making connections" between ideas or facts during the process of learning. The religious education facilitator should lead the process of discovery gently and clearly through a combination of questions and statements. This will help ensure the learner's continued sense of responsibility and add to feelings of success when the learner achieves a new level of understanding.

SUMMARY

A covenant is accepted with full anticipation of success by both parties. All important dimensions of the process should be included in the final copy. The timing of the meetings between the facilitator and the learner should be agreed upon in advance.

The eventual success or failure of the learning covenant is determined in the implementation process. The monitoring that the facilitator introduces to the situation is an added aspect. The purpose of monitoring is to assist in the implementation so that it will be as successful as possible.

The following points are important to the process as reviewed in this chapter:

1. Remember to support the learner in the process of transformation to self-direction.

2. Remember that the learner is responsible for implementation and the facilitator is responsible for monitoring the process of learning.

3. Ensure that the meetings are held in a manner and situation compatible with the learning process and the learner's requirements.

4. Obtain and keep necessary resources available for the learner.

5. Use good questions to ensure that the learner understands the content and avoids difficulties that interfere with the learning process.

An additional advantage of the successful learning covenant is found in the skills that the learner acquires during the process. The facilitator should do everything possible to nurture the learner's skills during the monitoring process.

MORE RESOURCES TO HELP YOU FOLLOW UP WHAT YOU HAVE LEARNED FROM THIS CHAPTER:

1. Malcolm S. Knowles, *Using Learning Contracts: Practical Approaches to Individualizing and Structuring Learning* (San Francisco: Jossey-Bass, 1986), 44–45.

2. Judith M. O'Donnell and Rosemary S. Caffarella, "Learning Contracts," in *Adult Learning Methods: a Guide for Effective Instruction*, ed. Michael W. Galbraith (Malabar, Fla.: Krieger, 1990), 148–156.

A clear description of the roles of the two parties is presented in these two books.

3. Malcolm S. Knowles, *Self-Directed Learning: A Guide for Learners and Teachers* (Chicago: Follett, 1975), 38–43, 44–55.

Knowles describes the new role of the educator most effectively in these pages.

4. R. E. Y. Wickett, *Models of Adult Religious Education Practice* (Birmingham, Ala.: Religious Education Press, 1991), 106–107.

There are brief comments on these issues in this chapter by Wickett.

5. Allen Tough, Virginia Griffin, Bill Barnard, and Donald Brundage, *The Design of Self-Directed Learning*, ed. Reg Herman (Toronto: Department of Adult Education, Ontario Institute for Studies in Education, and Ryerson Polytechnical Institute, 1980) This is a package of print and videotaped materials.

See especially the videotape component with Bill Barnard, the facilitator who is in conversation with Lew Lewis, with reference to the issue of covenant monitoring.

It is important to remember that most resource materials spend too little time discussing this important process of implementation and monitoring. It will be difficult to discover the few good points that are contained in the literature. Do not be afraid to look carefully at the documents listed here.

7

EVALUATING THE
LEARNING COVENANT

Effective closure is important to any successful learning process. This chapter describes how the learning covenant can be concluded satisfactorily for the learner. It also considers the implications of any institutional or community requirements for the learning covenant.

If religious educators are to operate within the "spirit" of the learning covenant, they must avoid the limitations of many of the testing procedures that characterize other forms of education. The learning covenant model frees both learner and facilitator from certain traditional limitations such as written examinations.

There are two important perspectives to the process of evaluating learning covenants. The learner considers the results from the unique viewpoint that he brings to the situation. The religious education facilitator brings a somewhat different viewpoint that reflects both her unique experience and the responsibilities of the educator to the learner and any institutional or community requirements.

There are two dimensions to learning covenant evaluation that must be considered: (1) the evaluation of the substantive content of learning that has occurred, or what some people may refer to as the "results" of the learning, and (2) the process of learning, namely, the "how" the learning occurred, sometimes called the structural context. The first dimension is critical to the closure of the learning covenant activity. The second dimension assists both learner and religious educator to work more effectively in future learning activities.

We need to consider the types of information that enable us to evaluate the results of the learning in order to meet the requirements of both learner and religious educator. This includes the institutional requirements that the religious educator may be required to insert into the evaluation.

The nature of the evidence that is to be used by both the learner and the facilitator to evaluate the learning experience should be agreed in advance and contained in the covenant document. This evidence should assist the learner to consider the results of the process and should meet any additional requirements agreed to by learner and facilitator.

No valid evaluation may occur without reference to criteria. These criteria should be developed and agreed in advance and contained in the written covenant document. The learner and facilitator will then apply these criteria to the evidence that has been accumulated and presented.

It is also important to evaluate the covenant learning process itself. An individual learner who is growing in skills for continuous learning needs to reflect upon the effectiveness of the process, particularly his part in it. A religious educator can continue to develop skills for supervision while assisting the learner's skills to develop further through a process of sharing insights.

Another issue concerns those who participate in the evaluation process. I include the learner, the religious education facilitator, other learners (in group situations), external experts, and other knowledgeable persons, for example, persons who could be recipients of a newly acquired skill. The learner should receive the information from the other parties and share it with the facilitator.

CONTENT EVALUATION

This section reviews the specific ways in which substantive content can be evaluated appropriately in order to respond to the learner's requirements and, if necessary, to any institutional requirements. Because the content to be evaluated has been identified previously, our concern in this section is to ensure that the evaluation procedures are *consistent* with the content and process of the learning.

All important aspects of the substantive content must be evaluated. It is not sufficient to evaluate certain relatively important substantive content areas while neglecting others. Consider each area of substantive content to determine that it is receiving some consideration in the evaluation process.

It may be appropriate to allocate more time and activity to the evaluation of important aspects of the substantive content, but this is a decision to be taken jointly by the learner and the facilitator. The religious education facilitator should help to set priorities that reflect the learner's insights, which are based on his requirements.

The Nature of Evidence

Learning covenants allow learners to be creative in the type of evidence that they use and share with the religious education facilitator. Many learners have positive feelings about the flexible characteristic of learning covenants, but they may be uncertain about what is required.

The religious education facilitator should remember that a written document is not the only vehicle for expressing the results of learning. Some learners may be intimidated by the need to provide written evidence and would welcome the opportunity to explore other options.

A discussion of the ways in which evidence can be presented will assist the learner to consider various options. The following ideas may be helpful to the learner:

a. Written paper (research paper, learning journal, case study)

b. Demonstration or simulation (live performance)

c. Specific product (written, artistic, electronic media)

d. Oral evaluation (discussion)

e. Formal examination paper (classroom or take home)

The formal examination paper is most popular with many learners and is consistent with the original academic model of contract learning. A number of examples have been included within certain categories. The following paragraphs clarify these options through descriptions and examples.

There are several types of written documents that can be submitted. The research paper integrates literature and the results of other activities quite effectively, but it may not be acceptable or appropriate for a number of personal or other reasons. Learning journals are useful and effective because they introduce the element of personal learning; the case study approach allows a focus on the specific substantive content.

A research paper may appeal to learners and religious education facilitators who do not wish to stray far from the more traditional academic approaches to learning and evaluation. Those who choose it tend to be familiar with its requirements. Most alternative forms of evaluation fit with this alternative educational model and help the learner to accept the newer approach to learning.

Learners should keep good notes of their activities throughout the covenant process in order to ensure that they can produce a comprehensive document at the end. References and other information may be hard to locate or to remember in sufficient detail after the fact.

Learning journals can provide a thorough review of both the substantive content that has been learned and the process that has been used to enable the learning. Journals have proven effective for many alternative models in adult education and adult religious education. My own use of journals in learning covenants and other types of evaluation procedures has convinced me of their value.

Learners should be encouraged to work on their journals in conjunction with the overall ongoing learning process. Regular entries, which are written a short time after learning activities, capture immediate reactions and details of activities. Other entries may be written after time for reflection has been added to the learning process.

A case study focuses the learner's attention on the factual detail of the learning. It permits the learner to write a document that is less "academic" in the minds of many learners while avoiding the personal element of the journal.

Similar concerns apply for the learner about the notes that are to be kept. The major difference between case studies and research papers is found in the literature requirement. In learning covenants, a literature review need not be included in the case study paper.

Demonstrations or simulations are exciting for the learner who wishes to demonstrate newfound skills. To perform in a live situation or in a simulated context challenges both learner and facilitator. The decision to use a live demonstration or simulation should be based on the appropriateness of the approach to demonstrate the results of learning.

Certain learners like to have some kind of formal examination to demonstrate their learning, and some institutions require a formal examination experience for certain programs. Two types of "formal" examinations have been used for many years: oral and written types of examinations. An "informal" approach to the formal examination can reduce anxiety in advance of the activity.

The most popular form of evidence of learning for many learners is the "product" that somehow represents the result of their activities. This product should be consistent with the substantive content of the learning. Often it is derived directly from the process of learning.

Learners may submit evidence of their learning in the form of a product that is consistent with the substantive content. If someone is learning to make something or do something, the product may be the specific item that is produced. In my own courses, learners have wanted to develop curriculum materials or evaluation instruments as evidence in order to demonstrate the results of their learning about the design of curriculum materials or evaluation instruments.

A written product may be appropriate for certain forms of evidence of accomplishment. If a learner wishes to acquire skills that are best demonstrated by a written product, this type of product could be most useful to the evaluation process. Why should someone write a detailed series of points rather than create the product that illustrate the points?

If a learner wishes to develop skills to create evaluation questionnaires for use with learning groups in a faith community, the best evidence of accomplishment might be a well developed questionnaire. If a learner wishes to acquire program planning skills, the best evidence might be a design for an educational program. Why should someone write about a series of points of good program design when these skills can be demonstrated directly through application?

Other creative forms of product may be used in appropriate circumstances. Consider the possibility of photographs, poetry, painting, or sculpture. Would any of these items express the substantive content that has been learned in a more creative, insightful manner? Perhaps an item from this group could be combined with a written report or other item.

The electronic media offer more options. Audiotapes and videotapes may be suitable for certain forms of evidence that are best understood through the ear and eye and possibly through repetition.

Where skills in pastoral work or other "people skills" are concerned, tapes of interchanges may provide very helpful evidence. The videotape or audiotape may be used during the learning process as well, thereby providing an experience that will reduce nervousness in final taping sessions.

Discussions or oral examinations work well for learners with good oral skills. This form of examination may be quite informal and nonthreatening if the facilitator can adopt a conversational approach. Carefully constructed questions may be asked in a friendly tone to put the learner at ease while meeting the requirements of the situation. Both substantive content and process questions may be included in this evaluation process.

Written examinations should be used only if the learner prefers them or an accrediting agency requires them. The vast majority of adult learners do not prefer a written examination, so it should be avoided most of the time. In-person or take-home examinations are also options. Questions must be clear and consistent with the learning that has occurred.

Religious educators using the learning covenant model should remember that more than one form of evidence may be submitted. A combination of the previously described options may be suitable. Do not be afraid to try the alternative forms of evidence. They have been used with success in many universities as well as in other settings.

CRITERIA OF EVALUATION

The criteria for evaluation are used to determine the extent to which learning has occurred. The primary purpose of the development of criteria is to give the learner a clear perspective on the results of the learning process.

A key issue for criteria is the background that the learner brings to the learning situation. The extent of learning may be determined by the nature of prior learning and by additional learning achieved through the learning covenant.

The learner may identify specific criteria that he or she regards as important, which will have been discussed for clarification and understanding by the facilitator and added to the learning covenant

THE EVALUATORS

The burden of evaluation need not be assumed solely by the religious educator. The learning covenant model provides the opportunity to use other sources of evaluative information in important ways. Both the learner and the facilitator have important roles in this model, but valuable assistance is provided by other persons with expertise and by nonexperts with specific ways of contributing to the learning.

The evaluators of learning covenants may include the following persons: (1.) learner, (2.) facilitator, (3.) external experts, (4.) nonexperts with relevant experience. The following paragraphs describe the role played by each person in the process of evaluation.

The learner is central to the evaluation process in the learning covenant model. No one else, with the possible exception of the most sensitive religious education facilitator, will be more aware of the factors that motivate the learning process. The learner's perspective on the learning process also includes the feelings and reactions that have been central to the activities of the learning covenant.

Because the religious education facilitator was not with the learner at all times during the process of learning, the learner can provide information during the evaluation process that explains or clarifies situations. The evaluation process should be seen as a *partnership* between learner and facilitator.

The learner should coordinate information that has been received from other sources and information about what he knows about the learning covenant that was created cooperatively. Through the integration of external information and her own input, the religious education facilitator should assist the learner to see the totality of evaluative information. The facilitator should provide *perspective* and *understanding* to the evaluative process.

The external expert may provide evidence of learning through the assessment of a "product." Because religious education facilitators are not the sole sources of expertise on a topic, valuable information may be received from the external expert. This person is usually involved as a resource person during the learning process. In my own use of the learning covenant model, I normally request a written statement that is shared with the learner.

Religious educators should not discount the input of other persons without the traditional forms of expertise. There are persons who may be performing the skills to be acquired or may have some knowledge or background of relevance without being identified as experts. These persons may be engaged in covenants.

It is normally the facilitator's responsibility to help the

learner identify these nonexperts. The specific evaluative information that these persons provide should be included with the other evaluative information.

EVALUATING THE PROCESS

Both the learner and the religious education facilitator may wish to improve their performance. They can do this most effectively by taking time to discuss the learning process. A discussion is typically preferred over other methods because learners do not always want to write more; a discussion with prior notice and consideration may do the job very effectively.

The following questions provide a good basis for the discussion:

a. What were the most effective and useful parts of the learning for you?

b. What caused problems for you during the learning process?

c. How could I have provided more or better support for the learning process?

There are other questions to be asked for individual covenants as well as "probes" for the questions listed above.

SUMMARY

The evaluation process ends the experience of learning for all parties to the covenant. A successful learning covenant requires both parties to do the following:

1. Evaluate both the content and the process.

2. Consider a variety of forms of evidence, including a written paper, demonstration or simulation, oral examination, or specific products, before choosing one.

3. Do not limit your choice to only one method of evaluation if more than one may be used effectively for different aspects of the learning.

4. Use appropriate criteria to evaluate the learning.

5. Involve eternal experts and other persons, where appropriate, in the process of evaluation, as well as the learner and the facilitator.

Remember that the success of the learning process is important to learners; assist them to feel positive in appropriate ways about their experience.

MORE RESOURCES TO HELP YOU FOLLOW UP WHAT YOU HAVE LEARNED FROM THIS CHAPTER:

1. John L. Elias, *The Foundations and Practice of Adult Religious Education*, rev. ed. (Malabar, Fla.: Krieger, 1993), 270– 278.
See this section for an overview of evaluation in adult religious education.

2. Egon G. Guba and Yvonne S. Lincoln, *Effective Evaluation: Improving the Usefulness of Evaluative Results through Responsive and Naturalistic Approaches* (San Francisco: Jossey-Bass), 1987.
This book is a good general reference work for evaluation in education.

3. Malcolm S. Knowles, *Using Learning Contracts: Practical Approaches to Individualizing and Structuring Learning* (San Francisco: Jossey-Bass, 1986), 30–32, 78–79 (methods of evaluation and criteria), 84–85 (self evaluation), 88–89 (evidence), 106–110 (sample).

4. Malcolm S. Knowles, *Self-Directed Learning: A Guide for Learners and Teachers* (Chicago: Follett, 1975), 56–58, 81–91, 110–111.

Please see the preceding books (especially the specified pages) for Knowles' views on evaluation.

5. R. E. Y. Wickett, *Models of Adult Religious Education Practice* (Birmingham, Ala.: Religious Education Press, 1991), 66–73, 100–110.

This volume contains short references to the issues of evidence and criteria for evaluation, self-assessment, and types of evidence for covenants by content types.

8

USING LEARNING COVENANTS WITH GROUPS

The covenant process can be used very effectively with a group of people who have overlapping individual interests. The group may provide valuable support for the learning process of the individual. Sometimes the religious education facilitator may work more efficiently and effectively with a number of learners simultaneously.

It is important for all religious educators to remember that each person has an individual learning covenant and learns according to the process of his own covenant. The group can support the facilitative process of planning, monitoring, and sharing; however, the learner must prepare for and engage in the covenant process individually.

The group approach should only be taken if there are several learners with common areas of learning needs. If these learning needs coincide to a very high degree, another educational model may be more appropriate. If the needs have limited overlap, this approach can provide a sound basis for limited cooperation.

Groups should not be used to develop and conduct covenant learning if there is no coincidental substantive content or if the learner has need of considerable special attention. Coincidental substantive content provides a basis for the cooperation between learners that makes the group work harmoniously and effectively. Learners with special requirements, such as an inability to work in groups due to extreme shyness or limited learning skills, should be given appropriate individual attention by the facilitator.

GROUP PROCESS

The group process is most effective when the individual learner's needs are paramount. The role of other people involved in the group process, including both the facilitator and the other group members, is to support the learning through the covenant process.

Figure 8.1 provides an overview of the group process for learning covenants.

Figure 8.1: The Covenant (in a group)

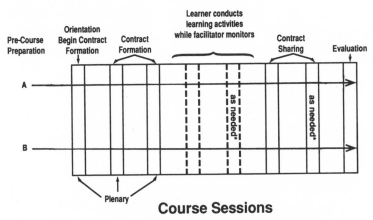

* "As needed" refers to holding sessions as required
by learners and the demands of contracts.

The following components for the process of a group covenant process should be considered:

a. Advance preparation

b. Group orientation to the covenant model

c. A group support system for covenant preparation

d. A system for group support of the individual covenant process

e. A process for sharing the results of the individual covenants

These components work coincidentally with the individual components of covenant learning.

ADVANCE PREPARATION

The group process is enhanced considerably by advance preparation on the part of learners. It is helpful to the process if all learners have a basic understanding of the nature of covenant learning at the outset. There are materials that can be read prior to the first session, and discussions may be held with those who are in need of the support that comes with personal reassurance. Because the covenant process is a new experience for many learners, it may be necessary to meet to discuss their concerns.

Malcolm Knowles's books on the subject of learning contracts may be used for advanced reading. Pages 25–28 in the book *Self-directed Learning: A Guide for Learners and Teachers* provide a short introduction. A more recent source of introductory information from Knowles is found on pages

27–36 in *Using Learning Contracts: Practical Approaches to Individualizing and Structuring Learning.*

Other readings for an introduction to covenant learning include R. E. Y. Wickett's chapter on learning covenants in *Models of Adult Religious Education Practice* and "Contract Learning and the Covenant" in *Adult Education and Theological Interpretations.* This latter volume is for those who desire a more extensive introduction to the concepts.

The religious education facilitator must remind the learners that this is a learning covenant and not a contract, particularly not a legal contract in any sense of the word. This particular view of learning covenants emphasizes the religious aspect of the spirit that guides the activity.

GROUP ORIENTATION

This orientation ensures that all learners have a basic understanding of the process for learning in covenants and for the group itself. Preliminary readings may raise questions in the minds of learners. Learners may desire clarification of the readings and they may seek the facilitator's perspective.

Appropriate introductory exercises should be used to ensure that learners are comfortable with the group and its setting. Such exercises may be found in writings about group activities in the annual editions produced by Pfeiffer and Jones and in writings by Hedley Dimmock and others.

A brief introduction to the concept of individual learning through the covenant process should follow the normal process of personal introductions. This introductory session is an important time to stress the need for covenants that conform to the spirit of learning as opposed to a legalist approach to learning. It will be helpful to Christians to explain the difference between biblical covenants in the Old Testament and the New Testament.

The introductory session is a good time to discover the various areas of interest within the group. This assists in the organization of learning partnerships which are to be discussed in the next section of this chapter. Group members may be asked to identify the area in which they wish to work on their learning covenant during the introductions.

GROUP COVENANT PREPARATION

We are concerned in this section with the requirements of the learning covenant and the appropriate group support that enables the learning covenant to be created. The process of development of the learning covenant was reviewed in chapter 3. This section focuses on the group support system for this developmental process.

First Meeting: Learning Covenant Formation

Documents from previously completed learning covenants may be shown to the group to illustrate the nature of a learning covenant. Chapters 9–11 of this book contain sample learning covenants that may be shared with the appropriate groups or individuals. This examination may be done in the plenary if the group has a small number of participants (six or fewer). Each person needs to have a copy of a sample learning covenant.

If the group has more than six members, the sample documents may be examined by subgroups of two followed by further discussion in the plenary. Each subgroup should be provided with a sample document. Subgroups may trade documents during the examination process. The religious education facilitator should attempt to provide each member or subgroup with a copy of a learning covenant that is as close as possible to the interests of the individual learner or subgroup.

The next activity involves learners' attempts to describe the area in which they want to learn and any ideas that they may have about resources or processes for learning. If the covenant group is small in number (six or fewer), the plenary will be an appropriate context for the discussion. Larger groups should divide into learning partnerships (described later in this chapter).

All learners should have an opportunity to share their ideas about the proposed learning covenant during this initial meeting. These ideas will be clarified during a process of discussion and questioning. Learners should be encouraged during this session to limit the proposed learning covenant to a manageable size. Potential resources may be identified by the learner, the religious education facilitator, and the peer group.

Learners should leave this meeting with a clear sense of the nature of learning covenants, the general nature of their own proposed learning, and some potential resources. They need to understand that they will be developing a draft of a learning covenant and to have an awareness of how to obtain any necessary assistance.

Additional Meetings:
Learning Covenant Formation

Forming a learning covenant will take longer for learners who are less familiar with this part of the process. Two additional meetings will be required, particularly for first-time participants in this model. The first such meeting involves sharing a draft of the learning covenant. The second meeting involves a review of the final document with the possibility of minor revisions and final approval.

The draft should be discussed by the group or subgroup in a manner that is supportive and positive for the learner and her efforts. The purpose of the critique is to ensure that the learner has an appropriate learning covenant to guide the learning process. Failure to achieve this result will ensure numerous difficulties along the way.

The difficulties that the group should consider in the learning covenant include the following:

a. A learning covenant that is too large or complex for the learner's situation or requirements

b. Inadequate resources

c. An inappropriate process, or flow, to the learning

d. Inadequate evaluation procedures and criteria

e. Inadequate evidence to satisfy the criteria

Earlier chapters refer to these and other difficulties in individual situations.

Learners should leave the final formation meeting with a

sense of confidence and the knowledge that their learning covenant is appropriate. This is a time to celebrate!

GROUP SUPPORT FOR INDIVIDUAL COVENANT LEARNING

A system of extended support is possible within the group learning situation. Learners should be aware that their learning will be enhanced through the cooperative process. Group support will help them to learn more about covenant learning and will assist them in their own specific learning process.

Group support is experienced in the plenary sessions and the subgroup sessions. This latter situation normally involves a group of two persons or a "learning partnership."

The plenary session supports learning through the general discussion of learning covenants and the specific discussion of individual learning covenants. A clearer picture of expectations and the nature of the covenant process is gathered in the plenary discussions. The sharing of individual proposals and results often yields further learning.

Learning partners meet in pairs. They can support each other in subgroup sessions on a one-to-one basis in the group setting and at other times. It is often helpful to share with someone who is going through a similar experience. Both positive and negative experiences can often be shared more easily with a peer.

Learning partners can assist in covenant formation at the early stages of the process. This guarantees an immediate and direct response to the learner's ideas. Both the facilitator and the partner can provide responses to the learner's questions and concerns during covenant formation.

The meetings of the monitoring process (see table 8.1) should be held with learning partners as well as others who wish to attend. It may be helpful to allow all who wish to attend monitoring sessions to do so with a clear understanding that certain learning partners are scheduled. Those individuals whose meetings are scheduled for that time should receive attention first, followed by the problems of others.

The nature of the content of the partners' learning covenants may suggest that they report the results of their learning at the same session of the plenary. This will ensure that related substantive content areas are covered in the same session.

SHARING THE RESULTS OF COVENANT LEARNING

The learners should return to the plenary session with all other members when the learning process has been completed and they are prepared to share the results of their learning activities. These sessions should be organized in advance for a time when the learners will have completed the learning activities.

In order for the sharing process to have the maximum effectiveness, learners' presentations should focus on the important things that they have learned. Presentations should avoid a lecture format and should enable discussion and inquiry. Evidence may be presented in a creative manner, as suggested in chapter 7. Learners who have studied similar content areas should be grouped together for their presentations.

THE ROLE OF THE FACILITATOR

The religious education facilitator must work with individual learners as well as with the group as a whole. This involves supporting the learner in all phases of the process, from developing the learning covenant to sharing the results of learning. This is consistent with the model of individual learning covenants. The religious education facilitator working with a group encourages the learners to become facilitators of each other's learning during the group sessions and at other times. Steps that can be taken are also listed in *Models of Adult Religious Education Practice.*

The formation of learning partnerships and the process of group sessions will simultaneously contribute to peer group support. The religious education facilitator's role is central to both activities. Using a sheet of newsprint, an overhead projector, or a blackboard, the facilitator can identify interests and assist learners to meet those with related interests. The facilitator should suggest that people with common interests discuss their work together.

THE ROLE OF THE PEER GROUP

Many peer group members can provide excellent ideas about the substantive content and the structural process of a covenant in the plenary or in the meetings of learning partners. Peers will frequently be aware of community resources that other group members may find helpful.

It is important that the religious educator impress upon group members that their role also is to support the other learners.

Their comments, like the religious educator's, should be supportive and helpful. The religious educator can demonstrate the value of questioning in the process of clarification. Suggesting resources is not demanding that resources be used but identifying a resource and considering the possibility of its use.

SUMMARY

The following points will enable the facilitator to use group sessions effectively in the support of learning covenants:

1. Groups can support individual learning through the covenant model provided that individual learning is recognized as paramount.

2. Groups can be oriented to the process of covenant learning through advanced reading and an introductory group session.

3. Learning partners and groups can work together to support the development of learning covenants.

4. Learning partners can attend monitoring sessions together.

5. The sharing of learning can be done in a group setting with reference to common areas of content.

Groups may differ in their operations; however, it is important to remember that a religious education facilitator and learning group who follow the above suggestions will maintain a high level of congruency with a model that is intended to support the individual.

MORE RESOURCES TO HELP YOU FOLLOW UP WHAT YOU HAVE LEARNED FROM THIS CHAPTER:

1. R.E.Y. Wickett, *Models of Adult Religious Education Practice* (Birmingham, Ala.: Religious Education Press, 1991), 108–109.

This book contains a description of the steps to follow in using the learning covenant model with groups.

2. Hedley G. Dimmock, *Groups: Leadership and Group Development,* rev. ed. (San Diego, Calif.: University Associates, 1983).

This book is an excellent resource for more information about the ways in which groups function and the ways in which they can be helped to work effectively.

3. Malcolm S. Knowles, *Self-Directed Learning: A Guide for Learners and Teachers* (Chicago: Follett, 1975), 46–58.

4. Malcolm S. Knowles, *Using Learning Contracts: Practical Approaches to Individualizing and Structuring Learning* (San Francisco: Jossey-Bass, 1986), 9–13.

Malcolm Knowles provides a set of procedures for working effectively with groups. His earlier book contains specific suggestions in one section, whereas the later book has suggestions interspersed throughout. I have noted the basic outline for a group from the later book in the following recommendations.

5. Judith M. O'Donnell and Rosemary S. Caffarella, "Learning Contracts," in *Adult Learning Methods: A Guide for Effective Instruction*, ed. Michael W. Galbraith (Malabar, Fla.: Krieger, 1990), 140–144, 150–153.

O'Donnell and Cafarella discuss the use of learning contracts in workshops, seminars, and conferences for group audiences, although much of the discussion focuses on work with individual learners.

9

LEARNING COVENANTS
FOR LAY MINISTRY

Lay ministry refers to work that is performed in many faith communities by members of the community who are not ordained. Many faith communities see this form of ministry as vital to the ongoing life of their group and may assign important responsibilities to laypersons with particular skills and knowledge.

No assumption about prior education and experience should be made with respect to each and every form of lay ministry. Some members of the faith community may have education or life experience that is highly relevant to a particular vocation to ministry, whereas others may have no education or experience relevant to the particular form of ministry in question. The selection and preparation of individuals and groups for lay ministry requires careful thought and appropriate action.

This chapter focuses on the work of ministry that lay members perform either as volunteers or as professional, paid staff within the context of the faith community. Volunteers perform the work of ministry without financial remuneration in spite of the importance of their work in the context of the total ministry of the faith community. Some lay ministry is paid because of the context and manner in which it must be done.

The learning covenant for lay ministry may involve group or individual learning situations. The nature of what is to be learned will be quite diverse in many faith communities. A full examination of the context and the learner's individual situation will enable a better understanding of the requirements of the situation.

AREAS OF LEARNING COVENANTS

The potential for covenant learning may be as diverse as the nature of lay ministry in the faith community. It is important for the religious educator to understand the nature of the lay ministry within the particular faith community and the subsequent areas in which learning will occur in order to function effectively in relation to the learner and the learning covenant.

The learning covenant for personal development is reviewed in chapter 11. This chapter (chap. 9) focuses on what may be referred to as the work of lay ministry, which includes all appropriate areas of responsibility that enable the faith community to conduct its ministry to members and others.

Many faith communities involve the laity in independent roles, whereas others require close supervision or team membership for laypersons in ministry. If there is to be supervision or team ministry involvement, the learning covenant facilitator should be aware of the nature of the context in which the ministry is to be performed in order to enable effective working relationships.

A religious education facilitator needs to know the basic areas of responsibility of lay ministers and the specific area in which the learning covenant activity is to occur. A learner enhances the effectiveness of the facilitator through the information provided to that person.

THE ROLE OF THE LAY LEARNER

It is important for the religious education facilitator to take into account the situation of the lay minister in relation to either full-time or part-time volunteer performance of ministry. Far from implying any less commitment on the part of the individual, this statement simply contextualizes the learning. A volunteer who has a full-time job will have limited time and energy for his or her learning in relation to ministry, whereas the persons whose role in ministry is full-time and paid will have more time and energy to commit to the learning covenant.

The learning of the layperson in ministry will occur most effectively in a cooperative and committed context. The lay learner in ministry needs to bring appropriate attitudes and abilities to the learning situation.

If the learning covenant activity is to be successful, the learner should have an attitude that accepts the value of self-directed learning. The learner should have confidence in an approach to learning that does not require the religious educator to provide all knowledge and skills to be acquired. In the absence of this confidence, the first-time learner should have a willingness to explore the value of self-direction.

The learner in ministry needs to have some understanding and skills in order to support the effectiveness of the learning process. The following list reflects these areas:

a. The learner should understand the nature of self-directed learning and the relevance of this approach to his requirements.

b. The learner should see herself as someone who does not need to depend on others for learning.

c. The learner should have the abilitiy to work with persons and resources to develop the learning plan and to undertake the process.

d. The learner should be able to take the initiative to identify and work with material and human resources.

e. The learner should be able to identify the relevant learning aspects of the learning process and to consider the results of the learning process.

THE ROLE OF THE FACILITATOR

The religious education facilitator's role with lay preservice or inservice preparation for ministry is based upon the broad range of learners who are chosen to participate in lay ministry. Certain faith communities have strong traditions of a broad base for ministry, whereas others focus on a limited "professional" base. The facilitator works with the group that is chosen to fulfil the role of lay ministry as defined by the faith community.

Another key issue for the religious education facilitator involves the learning skills of the individual learner. Although many professional clergy and laypersons have been exposed to individual learning activities in prior educational experiences, it is important to ensure that the learner who is to undertake the learning covenant possesses the required skills. A discussion with the learner should enable the facilitator to discover both the person's background and the person's level of confidence in these skills that enable the covenant process. Should the learner lack either skills or confidence, the religious education facilitator can support the learner's efforts to gain skill or confidence.

Readings and discussions can assist the process of skill development. A learner's confidence level is assisted by the same process of familiarization and eventual mastery of the required background.

The sample learning covenant included at the end of the chapter is typical of the type of covenant that a layperson with some experience and training will be able to produce with the support of an effective facilitator. It contains the major components of a normal learning covenant. It should not be regarded as a precise template of the learning covenant to be undertaken. The individual's background and the nature of the learning should determine the requirements of the situation.

The area of ministry to the sick, which includes visitation, is found in many Christian faith communities. It is an area where I have some experience in this area and have chosen it for illustrative purposes only. Each faith community must decide upon the role and function of the ministries to be assigned to lay and ordained persons.

Because learners have diverse backgrounds, simpler learning covenants may be chosen for work with certain individuals. Be flexible and work in a format appropriate to the learner.

Figure 9.1 Example of Learning Covenant for Laypersons: Ministering to the Sick

Learning Objectives	*Learning Resources and Strategies*
A. To develop an understanding of a Christian theological approach to illness, dying, death, and grieving	A1. Read (a) (b) (c) (d)
B. To develop the communication, prayer, and practical skills that are necessary to caring for the ill and grieving.	B1. Participate in the four-day volunteer training program with the pastoral care department at _____ or hospital, or pastoral home care services.
C. The ability to identify and utilize human, practical, scriptural, and prayer resources appropriate to different care-giving institutions.	C1. Same as B1.
D. To gain skill in relating to a care team, and working collaboratively.	D1. Learning resources E and F (Malcolm S. Knowles, *Self-Directed Learning*).
E. To become more aware of my abilities and limitations.	E1. Read _____ Myers-Briggs personality/profile or _____.

Figure 9.1 Continued

Learning Objectives	*Learning Resources and Strategies*
F. To become aware of the parish's and minister's needs, expectations, and requirements regarding ministry to the ill.	F1. Become involved in my parish boards regarding social ministry and meet with parish minister for consultation as required.

Evidence of Accomplishment	*Criteria and Means of Validating Evidence*
A. Annotated bibliographies of selected readings	A1. Open discussion with peers and mentor regarding readings to review clarity and understandings.
B. Performance as a helper and helpee in a care environment with two or more peers and pastoral care minister.	B1. Rating by peers and hospital pastoral care minister on my effectiveness as a helper and my openness to feedback as a helper
C. Same as B.	C1. Same as B 1
D. Performance as a helper and helpee with two or more peers and mentor.	D1. Rating by peers and mentor on my effectiveness as a helper and my openness to feedback as a helpee

Figure 9.1 Continued

Evidence of Accomplishment	Criteria and Means of Validating Evidence
E. Discussion with mentor regarding personal thoughts and results of tests.	E1. Role-playing various scenarios of caregiving experiences with peers with rating on my response effectiveness by peers and mentors
F. Same as learning resource and strategy in Knowles.	F1. Open discussion with other caregivers and the parish minister for feedbck on my effectiveness as a minister to the sick.

NOTE: If ratings are required (as on pages 62–63, learning resource C, of Knowles's *Self-Directed Learning* under "Criteria and Means of Validity Evidence") then I suggest ratings such as

*appropriateness
genuineness
usefulness
*effectiveness
empathy
practicality
*resource use (human etc.)

SUMMARY

The key points to remember from this chapter are:

1. Do not make assumptions about the prior experience and learning of the preservice or inservice lay learner.

2. Assist the learner to develop the skills required for individualized learning.

3. Remember the learner's variety of experience that is relevant to the growth of religious learning.

4 Support the development of the learner's skill level for covenant learning and the requisite feelings of confidence that enable learning.

5. Match the learning covenant to the individual situation.

MORE RESOURCES TO HELP YOU FOLLOW UP WHAT YOU HAVE LEARNED IN THIS CHAPTER:

These following publications contain a description of lay adult learning.

1. J. L. Elias, *The Foundations and Practice of Adult Religious Education* (Malabar, Fla.: Krieger, 1993), 101–107.

2. R. E. Y. Wickett and G. Dunwoody Learning Projects of Roman Catholic Adults in Early and Middle Adulthood. Insight, A Journal for Adult Religious Education 3 (1990): 64–71.

3. R. E. Y. Wickett, "Adult Learning and Spiritual Growth. *Religious Education*, 75 (1980) 452–461.

The following books contain descriptions of the abilities and knowl-edge that learners require to pursue a covenant approach.

4. Malcolm S. Knowles, *Self-Directed Learning: A Guide for Learners and Teachers* (Chicago: Follett, 1975), appendix B.

5. Malcolm S. Knowles, *Using Learning Contracts: Practical Approaches to Individualizing and Structuring Learning* (San Francisco: Jossey-Bass, 1986), 44.

A further suggestion for reading is that you familiarize yourself with the roles and functions of lay ministers within your own faith community. Material from other faith communities may also be helpful. Additional material that describes lay ministry in your faith community may be very valuable to the development of an understanding of the options for learning covenants. This material may be available in many faith communities, although it will vary in nature and content according to the nature of the faith community.

10

LEARNING COVENANTS FOR ORDAINED MINISTRY

Ordained ministry presents particular challenges for those who pursue it in the service of their faith communities. This form of ministry is demanding in many ways, but all manifestations of ordained ministry have one thing in common, the need for continuous learning.

Many faith communities appoint people to assume special responsibilities for ministry within their own particular context. The titles given to these persons vary, but they are distinguished from other members of the community by such factors as their roles and functions. Many faith communities require these ordained persons to have considerable training prior to assuming the role of ordained minister. Other faith communities emphasize other qualifications.

Important factors that we must consider include the prior learning of ordained persons and the nature of their employment within the faith community. Different faith communities have different forms of preordination training. Some forms of ministry are more general in nature, whereas others are more specialized. People accumulate various forms of experience through their life in ministry.

Most faith communities require a significant level of education prior to involvement in ordained ministry. Although the specific nature of education prior to ordination varies, this previous learning should be considered when learning covenants are developed. This consideration should include the content and the learning skills acquired through prior educational experience.

Many ordained persons are employed full-time by their faith communities, but others are not. Part-time or nonstipendiary ministry may necessitate limits on the commitment of time and energy to all aspects of work for the faith community, including the learning aspect. The work responsibilities of full-time ministry may also exert an impact upon learning commitments.

Persons who are ordained by their faith community normally have specific responsibilities within the context of the faith community that they serve. This chapter reviews the learning situation for the professional aspect of those responsibilities. I refer here to what we might call the "work" of ministry.

Many forms of ordained ministry are exercised in individualized settings or in contexts in which the ministry has features that are quite unique to the situation. Group and individualized learning opportunities must be explored to enable the person to perform the requisite role.

This chapter focuses on the learning covenants that support the learning of ordained ministers within the context of the faith community. The requirements of this special learning situation and the type of learning covenant that is most useful in this context are discussed in the following paragraphs.

The following issues are of critical importance to the implementation of the learning covenant model for professional, ordained ministry:

a. A clear focus on the content area of the proposed learning covenant

b. The appropriate process for working with an educated, competent professional with prior learning experience

c. Respect for the current knowledge, skills, and experience of the learner

AREAS OF LEARNING COVENANTS

I believe that learning covenants for those engaged in ordained ministry should have two specific dimensions: the professional and the personal. The former is critical to the performance of work related to the "profession" of ministry. The latter is critical to the maintenance of the individual's spiritual health that enables professional ministry to occur. Chapter 11 reviews the issues of the learning covenant for personal development. This chapter focuses on what may be referred to as the professional aspect of ministry. This work is defined differently in different faith communities and for different positions within the organization of each faith community.

In order to work effectively with the learner in the context of roles and responsibilities in the workplace, the facilitator needs to have a basic knowledge of the roles and responsibilities for ministry of the individual learner and of the specific area of ministry in which the learning will occur. These roles and responsibilities may be defined in such sources as formal job descriptions, letters of appointment, or other documents. A discussion of these roles and responsibilities will be helpful as the facilitator attempts to obtain basic information or to add to information from written documents.

The learner may wish to meet certain requirements for professional practice or certification. These "formal" factors should be taken into account when the covenant is developed. Documents that describe these qualifications should be reviewed by the facilitator as well as the learner prior to the development of the learning covenant.

WORKING WITH THE LEARNER

Working with well-qualified professionals in ministry has particular characteristics that differ from many other situations. These people are generally characterized as well-educated practitioners; and the way in which we work with them should be constistent with their levels of competence and training. The key word here is *respect* for their experience and competence.

There is a certain amount of sensitivity in our culture to the role of the person in the workplace and the competencies that enable the person to perform that role. Any discussions of that learner's role in the workplace with the learner or any other person who may be consulted should give due consideration to the need for confidentiality.

The general process to be undertaken involves the cooperative exploration of the learner's situation and the ways in which learning can support the more effective practice of ministry. A learning covenant should evolve naturally from the process of exploring of a specific dimension of the learner's ministry.

One approach that I have employed effectively with professionals as learners is to have them list their strengths and the areas in which they feel the need to gain more knowledge, skill, or understanding. This approach ensures that they enter the process with positive feelings and a clearer focus on what needs to be done.

THE ROLE OF THE FACILITATOR

The role of facilitator is one of a professional in relationship with another professional. It involves two forms of ministry, the ministry of the learner and your own commitment to an educational ministry. Both ministries will be more successful if the two parties are able to work in a cooperative manner.

The successful facilitator will begin to learn about the context of the learning situation in the first session. This will support the process of building a relationship with the learner that will support the process of continuous learning.

The facilitator's ability to provide input to content may be of importance to the learner in this situation. Your own knowledge may be tested, but it is still not essential to have all required knowledge, skill, or understanding. Your role as a partner in the planning, implementation, and evaluation parts of the process is more important. Remember that there are often considerable community resources within the faith community and beyond that may be very helpful in supplementing any content input by the facilitator. Resources that are sensitive to ecumenical and interfaith concerns can be most useful.

The role of the facilitator involves both the content to be learned and the ability to facilitate the learning process. The learning covenant included at the end of this chapter demonstrates the most complex form of covenant. Chapter 9 and chapter 11 provide simpler examples of learning covenants for learners who have different educational experiences or little background in this particular model.

Most persons who have been ordained have substantial educational experience in preparation for their ministry. Some may have experienced a form of this model during the educational process that preceded their placement in a position in a faith community or elsewhere. The example in this chapter was chosen to reflect both the complexity of some learning covenants and the Christian background of the author. Other faiths may choose to substitute references from their holy writings in place of references that are specific to a different faith. Should the specific content of this sample learning covenant be a concern in a faith community, other sample learning covenants are available.

SUMMARY

The following points will help you remember the key issues that were identified in this chapter:

1. The context of the particular ministry is vital to an understanding of the learning requirements of the learner.

2. Prior learning and experience may be critical to the learner's development of a learning covenant.

3. Confidentiality is important because the learner's work in ministry may involve very sensitive issues.

4 The learning covenant should be developed in the detail that will enable the learning.

5. Reference may be made to the "continuing education requirements" for learning when the circumstances require such reference to be made.

Figure 10.1 Example of Learning Covenent for Professional Ministry: The Bible in Contemporary Theology

Learning Objectives	Learning Strategies and Resources
A. Define the concept of "contemporary theology" from an analytical perspective.	A1. Required readings
B. Explore and analyze current church theology from the perspective of contemporary theology.	B1. Five selected readings on the issues of contemporary theology and biblical exegesis and church history.
	B2. Required readings
C. Interpret and distinguish major contemporary theologians.	C1. Required readings of works by Hall, Ruether, and Moltmann
D. Prepare a biblical exegesis from the perspective of contemporary theology	D1. Required readings of works by biblical scholars.
	D2. Required readings of selected biblical texts.
E. Describe historical events/persons that have influenced the development of contemporary theology in the church.	E1. Provide five resource references that are relevant to the development of contemporay theology and/or contemporary theology in the church.

Figure 10.1 Continued

Learning Objectives	Learning Strategies and Resources
F. Describe the implications of contemporary theology for biblical exegesis and for church theology.	F1. A debate between two randomly assigned teams: Team 1: Implications of contemporary theology for the Church Team 2: Maintaining traditional theologies in the Church F2. Required readings
G. Describe a personal theology in regard to contemporary theology	G1. Maintain a personal journal throughout course listing thoughts, reactions, notes, texts, bibliographic information, etc. G2. Development a personal theology using journal notes, readings, class work, etc.

Evidence of Accomplishment	Criteria and Means of Validating Evidence
A. A one- or two-page written definition of "contemporary theology"	A1. Assignment should be clear and concise. To be shared in open discussion with students. Submitted to professor for validation.
B. Submission of five annotated bibliographies	B1. Bibliographies will be clear and concise and will follow the required format. Validation by the expert.

Figure 10.1 Continued

Evidence of Accomplishment	Criteria and Means of Validating Evidence
C. Submission of a fifteen-page written paper on two or three contemporary theologians.	C1. Assignment and bibliography should be clear and concise and follow the required format. Validation by expert.
D. Submission of annotated bibliographies	D1. Bibliographies to be clear and concise in the required format. Validation by the expert.
Submission of textuals exegesi of two texts from required readings	D2. Exegesis to be clear and concise
E. Submission of annotated bibliographies on five chosen resources.	E1. Copy of annotated bibliographies to be circulated among students and used in open discussion. Validation by expert
F. Submission of eight annotated bibliographies. These bibliographies must include two references from both debate positions	F1. Bibliographies will be clear and concise and will follow required format. Validation by professor
G. Not to be submitted	G1. Not to be evaluated
Submission of a four- or five-page written paper.	G2. Assignment should be clear and concise and should follow required format. Validation by professor.

MORE RESOURCES TO HELP YOU FOLLOW UP WHAT YOU HAVE LEARNED IN THIS CHAPTER:

1. Malcolm S. Knowles, *Using Learning Contracts: Approaches to Individualizing and Structuring Learning* (San Francisco: Jossey-Bass, 1986), 162–163, and 180–196.

These pages describe the basic approach to professional development and provide an example of a learning covenant that a professional might create.

2. Judith M. O'Donnell and Rosemary S. Caffarella, "Learning Contracts," in *Adult Learning Methods: A Guide for Effective Instruction*, ed. Michael W. Galbraith (Malabar, Fl.: Krieger, 1990), 150–153.

This section provides specific examples of covenants for professional development.

3. Malcolm S. Knowles, *Self-Directed Learning: A Guide for Learners and Teachers* (Chicago: Follett, 1975), 62–63.

4. Malcolm S. Knowles, *Using Learning Contracts: Approaches to Individualizing and Structuring Learning* (San Francisco: Jossey-Bass, 1986), 71–74.

5. R. E. Y. Wickett, *Models of Adult Religious Education Practice* (Birmingham, Ala.: Religious Education Press, 1991), 104–105.

These pages provide information about the development of the relationship between learner and facilitator.

11

LEARNING COVENANTS FOR PERSONAL DEVELOPMENT

This chapter focuses on the individual personal development that occurs in the process of faith growth and change. We shall consider the ways in which learning covenants may support the learning of a person whose focus for learning activity is her own personal faith development.

This chapter is concerned with the learning that occurs for faith development for all individual persons, ordained or lay, in the faith community. The central focus is the type of learning and not the role or function within the faith community.

There is no doubt that this area of learning is important at any given time to many members of our faith communities and also to many beyond our groups in the larger community. Each person should be encouraged to consider the status and stage of his own faith development and the future potential for growth and change.

The various processes by which individuals engage in faith development are varied and complex in nature. Learning covenants may assist the learner in several ways, but the learning that occurs needs to be consistent with the broader issues of the individual's faith development process.

Learning covenants may occur in individual or group settings, but the focus of the learning covenant must always be the individual's requirements. The group can provide a suitable setting for support of the individual's learning.

Some faith communities choose to limit the areas in which they facilitate faith development, either for members of their own faith community or for others. The choice must be made in an appropriate manner within the faith community as to what does or does not fall within the specified limits for facilitation of learning. Facilitators would do well to consider these limits carefully when they appear to conflict with the learner's interests.

AREAS OF LEARNING COVENANTS

Learning covenants for individual faith development must reflect the requirements of the individual. The fact that the individual is part of a particular faith community will contribute to the direction and nature of the process of faith development.

Life experience is often seen as central to adult learning and development by experts in the area. This viewpoint may be projected on to the area of faith development. Religious educators need to consider the importance of life experience to the individual person's process of learning. The substantive content of a learning covenant radiates from the life experience of many learners. Both reflection and integration are required for effective learning that involves life experience and new forms of knowledge.

Many persons see the substantive content of the learning covenant in the context of a faith journey, or the process of growth and development that occurs during the individual's lifetime. That journey may be made on an individual basis, but the traveler may interact in various ways with other travellers along the path of the journey. Religious educators may understand the process of faith development more clearly if we are able to accept the analogy of the journey.

Many learners are motivated to learn through certain life experiences. Traumatic life experiences normally create a very serious need to learn. The learner's response to the need to learn may be dramatic and swift or it may be felt over time.

WORKING WITH THE LEARNER

Religious educators need to be aware of conditions that tend to lead to a successful learning experience. Each learner's unique response to a situation ensures that the most appropriate way to respond varies according to the requirements of the situation of each individual learner.

The following conditions of learning should exist for the learner if the learning experience is to be successful:

a. The learner feels a need to learn something.

b. An appropriate learning environment exists.

c. The learner is committed to the goals and direction of the learning experience.

d. The learner is involved in the planning process.

e. The learner is committed to the learning experience and is fully involved in it.

f. The learning process includes reference to the learner's prior experience.

g. There is progress in the learning process that satisfies the learner's requirements.

Successful support for learning requires attention to these conditions.

Learners also need to feel that the educator respects the way in which they approach learning in any substantive content area. Facilitators need to pay particular attention to support for less obvious means of learning and to the contribution that various life experiences make to the learning process.

Each learner's life experience has certain particular characteristics and dimensions that make it unique. Because people react differently to different experiences, it is important to respect the variety of factors that impact on each learner.

THE ROLE OF THE FACILITATOR

A facilitator in a learning covenant needs to consider the nature of the development that the learner pursues. A process of discussion with appropriate questioning will lead to a deeper understanding for both learner and facilitator.

The religious education facilitator needs to consider the various learning experiences that the learner wishes to have. These experiences should be consistent with the faith direction in which the learner intends to go and with the learner's ability to consider and understand the relevance of each learning experience to the faith development process.

The religious education facilitator would do well to remember that various life experiences carry different importance for different people. It is necessary to determine relative importance through discussion and questioning. The term "relative importance" refers to the learner's perspective on this issue. Something that may not appear important to a facilitator may be of considerable importance to the learner. The reverse may also be true at times, and the religious educator's suggestions may not resonate with the learner.

Flexibility and responsiveness are key to the work of the facilitator. Because of the diversity of learners and their backgrounds in this group, it is incumbent on the facilitator to adjust to the situation and play an appropriate role.

Although the pattern of learning covenants may be similar for certain groups of learners, each learning covenant is different because it reflects the individual. The religious educator should bear in mind that those who pursue learning for personal development have a variety of educational experience. The learning covenant that follows (fig. 11.1) is intended to provide one approach to the learning covenant. Chapters 9–10 provide examples of more complex covenants that may be used with more experienced learners.

These covenants are organized in a simple manner to avoid confusion in the process of covenant formation and to provide the most simple base for the written document. They include the essential elements needed to make the covenant effective for appropriate learners.

Figure 11.1 Example of Learning Covenant for Bible Study: The Gospels (Matthew, Mark, Luke, John)

Learning Objectives (Step 1)	Learning Activities (Step 2)
A. Be able to identify the differences and similarities between the four Gospel books.	A1. Read selected readings from four Gospel texts.
	A2. Confer with mentor once a week for a half-hour meeting for four weeks to discuss selected readings and Gospels.
B. Be able to identify a central Gospel message for each Gospel author: Matthew, Mark, Luke, and John.	B1. Read selected chapters from the four Gospels listed and other selected readings.
	B2. Meet with mentor once a one-hour meeting for six weeks to discuss readings.
C. Be able to identify a personal Gospel message from the combination of Matthew, Mark, Luke, and John and integrate this message with the theology of the New Testament as a whole, to you, personally, and within a Christian community.	C1. Keep a personal journal throughout learning objectives assignments 1 & 2.

Figure 11.1 Continued

Evaluation (Step 3)

A1a.   Describe three similarities and three differences among the four Gospels.

A2a.   Identify a specific Gospel message for each Gospel author.

A3a.   Outline a message that is found in all four Gospels and describe what this means with references to personal, theological, and faith community isues.

SUMMARY

The following key points will enable you to work more effectively with learners:

1. The content of learning for personal development is often as diverse as the many individuals who constitute the faith community, as well as those beyond its limits.

2. The processes of faith development through individualized learning can be complex and varied.

3. Learning must be seen as valuable and as leading to success for the learner to ensure full participation.

4. Use a form of covenant that suits the skills and knowledge of the learner.

5. Be prepared to be flexible and open to the various possibilities.

MORE RESOURCES TO HELP YOU FOLLOW UP WHAT YOU HAVE LEARNED IN THIS CHAPTER:

1. R. E. Y. Wickett and G. Dunwoody, "Learning Projects of Roman Catholic Adults in Early and Middle Adulthood," *Insight: A Journal for Adult Religious Education* (1990): 3 64–71.

2. R. E. Y. Wickett, *Adult Learning and Spiritual Growth, Religious Education*, 75 (1980): 452–461.

The following articles contain reviews of the learning activities that are related to religion in various ways. They demonstrate the diver-

sity of learning that may be encountered as adults pursue learning in this particular area of life.

3. John Elias, *The Foundations and Practice of adult Religious Education* (Malabar, Fla.: Krieger)(1993): 229–233.

John Elias comments on the nature of the "religious" content in his book on adult religious education.

4. Malcolm S. Knowles, *Self-Directed Learning: A Guide for Learners and Teachers* (Chicago: Follett) (1975): 46–58.

5. Malcolm S. Knowles, *Using Learning Contracts: Practical Approaches to Individualizing and Structuring Learning* (San Francisco: Jossey-Bass) (1986): 9–13.

The sections noted above of these frequently cited books support a deeper understanding of the lay learner's process of interaction with the facilitator.

12

SUMMARY

The reader should now have a sense of the nature, scope, and potential for the religious educational model of the learning covenant. This chapter summarizes the key points for the understanding and implementation of the learning covenant model. The challenge is to apply the principles with the learner in the context in which they are most likely to bring about a successful outcome.

The initial chapters introduced the important concepts of the model with a view to the theological and educational principles that support this approach to learning. The following chapters reviewed the specific methodology and the various types of learners who participate in the learning covenant process.

THE KEY ISSUES

The outlines of processes and examples that have been provided in the preceding chapters are not definitive but are intended to provide a general template against which the practitioner may consider his activities. Any educational model, method, or technique must be used with due regard for the situational context in which it used. A number of key issues emerged in the preceding chapters, and these issues are summarized in the following paragraphs.

The covenant model has its roots in the Judaeo-Christian

tradition within the various interpretations of the concept of the covenant. Covenants evolved as the "people of God" grew in their knowledge and understanding of God. For Christians and Jews alike, the model has important roots in the history and the theology of the two religions. It also has roots in other religious traditions that come from early civilizations.

It is important for the religious education facilitator establish a good working relationship with the learner. It is difficult to imagine any serious learning through the use of this model without due care and attention to the relationship between the adult learner and the facilitator. The facilitator must see the learner as a responsible, mature, committed person and must develop an appropriate relationship with the learner based upon that viewpoint.

The religious education facilitator should assist the learner to locate and use appropriate resources for the learning process. No learner is able to achieve the desired results without access to certain required human and material resources. The ability to locate and to use resources is an immense asset to the process of the learning covenant and is important to the continuous learning of the individual learner.

Assist the learner to become self-directed during the process of covenant formation through the development of a clear statement of purpose, adequate resources, and a strategy for learning with an appropriate timetable for the learning covenant. The skills that are identified with the learning covenant model are also valuable to the learner in the context of other religious educational procedures or any independent learning. As the facilitator enables the development of such learning skills, the learner can develop very useful skills for both short- and long-term learning activities.

Remember that the learner is responsible for implementing the covenant and the facilitator is responsible for monitoring the process of learning. There are two roles that can be clearly defined, and it is important for each party to respect the other's role in the learning process. The religious education facilitator remains aware of the process of learning through an appropriate monitoring process, while the learner can proceed according to the plan with confidence and the knowledge of the facilitator's support.

Evaluate both the substantive content and the substantive process through a variety of types of evidence, including written documents, demonstrations or simulations, oral examinations, or specific products that represent the results of learning. The learner will wish to bring closure to the learning experience in an appropriate way. A response by the facilitator to both the content and the process of the learning can help to provide the type of closure needed by the learner.

The learning covenant can be used effectively with both individuals and groups, but group sessions should focus on the learning requirements of each individual learner. This model fosters individual learning. When it is used in group settings, the group supports the learning of each individual. When group cohesion and cooperative learning are the goal, a sense of group will be created much more effectively through the use of other religious education procedures that are better suited to the development of group cohesion and cooperation. Learning partnerships are an effective means to support the group learning covenant process.

There are learning requirements for the different forms of ministry in various faith communities as well as certain individual needs that may be met through the use of this model. It is important to understand the context of ministry and personal growth in order to implement the model.

The type of ordained ministry and prior learning experience determine the nature of the learning covenant. The religious education facilitator needs to consider the learner's requirements and background in order to achieve a successful support role for the learning process. Because of the rich diversity of roles and functions for ordained clergy, a careful review of the current needs in the situation are vital. Similarly, the learner needs to take into consideration the breadth of his or her prior training and learning experiences in order to provide an appropriate beginning to the learning covenant process.

The type of lay ministry and prior learning experience determine the nature of the learning covenant. Lay ministry is incredibly diverse in nature, as are the backgrounds of those who are involved in lay ministry. In many situations, lay ministers are an even more diverse group, thus necessitating considerable preparatory work and various approaches to the facilitational role from the more supportive to the less supportive.

Learning covenants for personal development have the potential to be as broad as the human experience of the spiritual dimension. There are many learners for whom the faith journey is an exciting and important part of their lives. To share in the journey is a privilege with much responsibility. The learning covenant procedure enables both the sharing and the fulfilment of responsibility in a manner that is compatible with the learning situation of adults.

CONCLUDING THOUGHTS

The versatility and scope that the learning covenant procedure brings to the support of adult learning is considerable. Its contributions to the learning process are often seen during the specific learning activity that is undertaken with the facilitator *and* during those learning activities that follow.

We religious educators should never underestimate the importance of our role as educators nor should we overestimate it. We are not responsible for all learning that occurs for the learner, and we should not assume that learners will not take something away from their experience with us that will assist in their further learning.

The ability of this model to adapt to certain group learning situations is a definite plus. Religious educators should not hesitate to use it with groups that require individualized learning with both group participation and support.

Religious educators should adapt this educational model to the learning situation. We have to consider the learner, substantive content, human and material resources, and situational context, as well as our own skills and abilities, when we perform this task.

INDEX